VARMINT RIFLES
AND CARTRIDGES

Also by the Author

Cartridge Reloading in the Twenty-First Century

VARMINT RIFLES AND CARTRIDGES

A COMPREHENSIVE EVALUATION OF SELECT GUNS AND LOADS

Charles T. Richards

Skyhorse Publishing

Skyhorse Publishing books may be purchased in bulk at special discounts for sales promotion, corporate gifts, fund-raising, or educational purposes. Special editions can also be created to specifications. For details, contact the Special Sales Department, Skyhorse Publishing, 307 West 36th Street, 11th Floor, New York, NY 10018 or info@skyhorsepublishing.com.

Skyhorse® and Skyhorse Publishing® are registered trademarks of Skyhorse Publishing, Inc.®, a Delaware corporation.

www.skyhorsepublishing.com

10 9 8 7 6 5 4 3 2 1

Richards, C. T. (Charles T.)
  Varmint rifles and cartridges : a comprehensive evaluation
of select guns and loads / C. T. Richards.
       pages cm
  Summary: "A thorough guide, Varmint Rifles and Cartridges provides detailed information about getting started in varmint hunting, selecting the best rifles for the job, and choosing your cartridges and other components. The text is supplemented by more than one hundred detailed photographs that illustrate the various types of rifles and cartridges available for varmint hunters. Varmint Rifles and Cartridges presents information about the history of varmint hunting and how those original rifles differ from the most popular rifles and cartridges available for varmint hunters on the market today. Each chapter of the book is dedicated to a particular cartridge, including the: Ruger Remington Swift Winchester Roberts. At the end of each chapter, author C. T. Richards demonstrates how each cartridge and rifle performs through the results of range tests and trajectory tests he conducted himself. A varmint hunter since the 1950s, Richards is more than qualified to grade these products and offer advice on varmint hunting in general. The content of Varmint Rifles and Cartridges will appeal to readers considering varmint hunting for the first time, as well those who have previously acquired some experience in using these tools. "—Provided by publisher.
  ISBN 978-1-62636-558-2 (pbk.)
  1. Hunting rifles. 2. Bullets. 3. Varmint hunting. I. Title.
SK274.2.R53 2014
799.2028'32—dc23
                          2013034822

Printed in China

A well regulated Militia, being necessary to the security of a free State, the right of the people to keep and bear Arms, shall not be infringed.

— Second Amendment to the US Constitution

This book is dedicated to the memory of my good friend and shooting buddy, John Hulyo.

Contents

Preface

I first became a serious varmint shooter in the summer of 1950 at the ripe old age of 15. I bought my first center-fire rifle from the local sporting goods store—a Winchester Model 43 chambered for the then-popular .218 Bee. I also purchased and installed a Weaver J4 scope using Weaver bases and mounts. To this day, I still regret selling that rifle. The little Bee was also the cartridge that introduced me to reloading.

I have fond memories of my father driving me to a local dairy farm on a summer evening or, better yet, a Saturday morning to shoot woodchucks. I must admit, it took me a little while to get over woodchuck fever. But I soon started to make kills out to 150 yards or more. I was now a budding varmint shooter. There were no dedicated gun magazines back then, but I purchased any issue of *Outdoor*

A 1952 photo of the author with his Model 43 Winchester and a pasture poodle who succumbed to the sting of the Bee.

Life or *Field & Stream* that contained articles about varmint shooting. I soon became a fan of both Jack O'Connor and Warren Page.

My next varmint rifle was a .257 Roberts, which I had custom-built around a commercial FN Mauser action. After paying to have the rifle made, the only sight I could afford was a Lyman Model 48 aperture. No sooner was the rifle completed than I enlisted in the US Navy. To say my woodchuck hunting was interrupted is an understatement. Soon after my enlistment was up I married, which extended my absence from woodchuck hunting for another ten years, as my focus was on buying a home and raising a family.

Finally, in the late 1960s, I was able to resume my passion for shooting those pesky varmints. I installed a Leupold 3-9X variable on the Roberts and was able to make shots at more than 200 yards. I had also become friends with a coworker who shared my passion for sitting on the edge of an alfalfa field on a summer day and waiting for Mr. Woodchuck to stand up. We would take turns spotting and shooting. By that time my local farm had been sold to a developer, so we had to drive a little distance to find new pastures, but the trips were worth it.

The last rifle I actually hunted woodchucks with was a Ruger Model 77V chambered for the .220 Swift. I mounted a Leupold 12X fixed-power scope and, for me, that was the epitome of a varmint rifle. Now, no woodchuck was safe out to 300 yards!

I still have both the .257 Roberts and the Swift, and over time I have acquired more varmint rifles. But all of my shooting now is at paper targets at the local range. I get my satisfaction from shooting small groups with my handloaded ammo. I continue to experiment with different bullet and powder types, and I have settled on a few good loads for each caliber I shoot.

I have written this book to give prospective varmint shooters an idea of what is available today in the way of factory rifles and cartridges. It's a far cry from the few selections that were around when I first succumbed to varmint shooting fever. Not only are there a significant number of accurate varmint rifles available today, but factory ammo has also come a long way and can give serious competition to handloads. Each chapter in the book describes my relationship with a particular rifle in my collection and how that rifle performs at the range with both factory ammunition and handloads. I welcome anyone who is giving thought to purchasing a varmint rifle to join the fraternity. And to those who already enjoy the pastime, thank you for your dedication to the sport.

Chapter 1
Introduction

Varmint rifles mean different things to different people. In the Northeast, varmint rifles are used primarily to shoot woodchucks, also known as groundhogs, at distances of 100 yards and beyond. In the Southwest, they are used mostly to shoot the diminutive prairie dog at ranges in excess of 300 yards. Others use their varmint rifles to shoot the wily crow or coyote.

The true varmint rifle typically has a heavy barrel of at least 24 inches in length, a stock with a wide fore-end, and a trigger that's adjustable and often set to two pounds or lighter. However, many rifles used to shoot varmints do not match this configuration but are still quite practical. Some rifles do double duty as a varmint rifle and for shooting medium-size game, such as whitetail deer or antelope.

VARMINT RIFLES

The number of varmint rifles offered by major firearms manufacturers is an indication of how popular varmint shooting is today. When I purchased my first varmint rifle in 1950, a Winchester Model 43 in .218 Bee, the selection was much narrower. In perusing the 1951 edition of the Stoeger *Shooter's Bible*, the choices from Winchester were the aforementioned Model 43 in .22 Hornet or .218 Bee for $54.95 and the Model 70 in .22 Hornet, .220 Swift, .250-3000 Savage, or .257 Roberts for $123.25. If you wanted a heavier barrel and target-type stock, you could select the Model 70 Target Model in .220 Swift or .257 Roberts for $166.95. The Model 70 barrel length for the .220 Swift was 26 inches; it was 24 inches for all other calibers.

At that time, Remington offered its Model 722, the daddy of the present-day Model 700, in .222 Remington and .257 Roberts. By the way, this was the rifle that introduced the .222 Remington, which took the varmint shooting world by storm and for more than 20 years ruled the benchrest calibers. Like the Standard Model 70, the Remington Model 722 was a sporter-type rifle. The only other rifle choice was from Savage. It offered a Model 342 bolt action in .22 Hornet for an affordable price of $42.95 and a Model 99 lever action in .250-3000 Savage. There you have it—those were the choices back then, in both factory rifles and factory cartridges.

Handloaders had another option. You could have a rifle custom-built on a Springfield or Mauser bolt action, or one of the numerous single actions, such as the Winchester High Side Wall, and have it chambered for one of the many wildcat cartridges existing at that time. Some of the more popular wildcats were the .22 K-Hornet, the .219 Donaldson Wasp, and the .22-250 Varminter.

The most popular scopes for varmint shooting in the 1950s were the long target types with external adjustments. These were made by Fecker, Lyman, and Unertl. Powers ranged from 6X to 30X, depending on the brand. Also, internally adjusted scopes were becoming available at that time for both varmint shooting and big-game hunting. The most popular was the Weaver K-Series, which offered fixed magnification scopes from 2.5X (Weaver K2.5) to 10X (Weaver K10). Weaver was also one of the first to come out with a variable power scope, the Model KV (2¾X to 5X). The Weaver scopes were well-made, very good optically, and sold for a reasonable price. Other quality scopes having internal adjustments that a varmint shooter might consider were made by Lyman, Stith, Leupold, and Unertl.

Today, it's a totally different story. Not only do you have a wide selection of varmint rifles and scopes, but your choice of factory varmint cartridges is also quite extensive. I'm going to attempt to list what's currently available from gunmakers. Keep in mind, though, that this is a snapshot. Rifle models and cartridges appear and disappear based on their popularity.

Browning

Browning, based in Ogden, Utah, offers a number of high-quality rifles, including semiautomatic, lever-action, and bolt-action models. Their bolt-action series includes rifles built on both the A-Bolt and X-Bolt actions. The following models should be of interest to someone seeking a varmint rifle.

- **Model X-Bolt Varmint Stalker**—Features a composite stock with textured gripping surfaces, a medium-heavy free-floating barrel (24" for the .223 Remington and .243 Winchester, 26" for the .22-250 Remington), the X-Bolt action, and an adjustable three-lever Feather Trigger.

X-Bolt Varmint Stalker. Photo courtesy of Browning Firearms.

- **Model X-Bolt Varmint Special**—Features a green laminated thumbhole stock with cooling vents in the forearm, a glass-bedded receiver, a free-floating barrel (24" for the .223 Remington and 26" for the .22-250 Remington), the X-Bolt action, and an adjustable trigger. Varmint calibers include the .223 Remington and .22-250 Remington.

X-Bolt Varmint Special. Photo courtesy of Browning Firearms.

CZ-USA

CZ rifles are built in the Czech Republic and imported into the United States exclusively by CZ-USA. These are high-quality, accurate rifles that offer the varmint shooter choices in both a miniature Mauser-type-action 527 Series and a standard Mauser-type-action 550 Series.

- **Model CZ 527 Varmint**—Features a 24" heavy hammer-forged barrel, laminated or walnut varmint stock, five-round detachable magazine, and adjustable single-set trigger. The walnut-stock version is available in .17 Remington, .204 Ruger, and .223 Remington. The laminated-stock version is only available in .223 Remington.

CZ 527 Varmint Laminate. Photo courtesy of CZ-USA.

- **Model CZ 527 American**—Features a 24" hammer-forged barrel, Turkish walnut stock, five-round detachable magazine, and adjustable single-set trigger. This model is available in both right-hand and left-hand versions. The calibers available in the right-hand version are the .22 Hornet, .221 Remington Fireball, .204 Ruger, .222 Remington, and .223 Remington. The left-hand version

calibers are the .204 Ruger and .223 Remington. The **Model CZ 527 M1 American**, on the other hand, features a 24" hammer-forged barrel, Turkish walnut stock, 3-round flush-fit detachable magazine, and an adjustable single-set trigger. The M1 American is only available in .223 Remington. This model is also available with a synthetic stock.

CZ 527 American. Photo courtesy of CZ-USA.

- **Model CZ 550 Varmint**—The Model 550 features a standard-size Mauser-type action, 25.6" heavy barrel, four-round detachable magazine, and single-set trigger.

This model is available in a walnut, laminated, or Kevlar stock. The laminated stock features a ventilated fore-end. Calibers offered are the .22-250 and .308 Winchester.

CZ 550 Varmint. Photo courtesy of CZ-USA.

Kimber America

Originally founded as Kimber of Oregon, Kimber America is a relatively new firearms manufacturer that builds high-quality rifles known for their accuracy. The following Kimber varmint rifles all use the Model 84M action.

- **Model 84M Varmint**—Features a pillar-and-glass-bedded action, a 24" heavy sporter stainless-steel fluted barrel, a grade A walnut

stock, and an adjustable trigger. This model is available in .204 Ruger and .22-250 Remington.

Model 84M Varmint. Photo courtesy of Kimber America.

- **Model 84M ProVarmint**—Features a pillar-and-glass-bedded stainless-steel action, a 24" stainless-steel fluted bull barrel, a gray laminate stock, and an adjustable trigger. This model is available in .204 Ruger, .223 Remington, and .22-250 Remington.

Model 84M ProVarmint. Photo courtesy of Kimber America.

- **Model 84M Montana**—Features a pillar-and-glass-bedded action, a 22" sporter contour stainless-steel barrel, a Kevlar–carbon fiber stock, and an adjustable trigger. This model is available in .204 Ruger, .223 Remington, .243 Winchester, and .257 Roberts.

Model 84M Montana. Photo courtesy of Kimber America.

- **Model 84M LongMaster VT**—Features a pillar-bedded action, a 26" stainless-steel bull barrel, a gray laminated stock, and an adjustable trigger. This model is only available in .22-250 Remington.

Model 84M LongMaster VT. Photo courtesy of Kimber America.

Marlin Firearms

Marlin Firearms has been in existence since 1836 and is well-noted for its extensive line of lever-action rifles. In 2008, however, Marlin introduced the Model X7 Series bolt-action rifle. Included in this series is the Model X7VH. This rifle features a heavy 26" barrel, Marlin's Pro-Fire adjustable trigger, a fluted bolt, and a pillar-bedded synthetic stock. Also, a scope base is included with the rifle. The Model X7VH is offered in .22-250 Remington and .308 Winchester.

Model X7VH. Photo courtesy of Marlin Firearms.

Mossberg

Mossberg has been producing quality firearms since 1919. Its current rifle lineup is based on the relatively new Mossberg 4×4 action. The Mossberg MVP (Mossberg Varmint Predator) Series is built around the 4×4 action. With a rifling leade of 0.162", the Model MVP Series will safely accommodate the overall length of the 5.56mm NATO round—the military equivalent of the .223 Remington.

- **Model MVP Varmint**—Recently introduced by Mossberg, the Model MVP contains some unique features. These include: a target-style laminated stock, a pillar-bedded action with a spiral bolt, an adjustable LBA trigger similar to the Savage AccuTrigger, an AR-15-type magazine that holds 10 rounds of .223 Remington/5.56mm NATO ammo, and a bipod rest. This model is also available with a premounted and bore-sighted 4-15×50mm scope (the Model MVP Varmint-Scoped).

Model MVP Varmint-Scoped. Photo courtesy of O. F. Mossberg & Son, Inc.

- **Model MVP Predator**—Newly introduced by Mossberg, the Model MVP Predator contains many of the features of the Model MVP Varmint. The major differences are a laminated sporter-style stock and an $18\frac{1}{2}$" fluted medium bull barrel. The Predator is a good choice for a walking-around varmint rifle. Like the Varminter, it's also available in a scoped version (the Model MVP Predator-Scoped).

Model MVP Predator-Scoped. Photo courtesy of O. F. Mossberg & Son, Inc.

Remington Arms

Remington, America's oldest gun manufacturer, introduced the Model 700 rifle in 1962. This is an upgraded version of the Models 721 and 722, which it replaced. To this day, the Model 700 has been the mainstay of the Remington center-fire rifle lineup. Varmint rifle choices include the following models.

- **Model 700 VLS**—Features a laminated varmint-style stock, a heavy 26" barrel, and a trigger with adjustable pull weight. This model is offered in .204 Ruger, .223 Remington, .22-250 Remington, .243 Winchester, and .308 Winchester.

Model 700 VLS. Photo courtesy of Remington Arms Co.

- **Model 700 VL SS Thumbhole**—Features a laminated thumbhole stock with vents in the semi-beavertail fore-end, a stainless-steel 26" heavy contour barrel, and the X-Mark Pro trigger. This model is offered in .204 Ruger, .223 Remington, and .22-250 Remington.

Model 700 VL SS Thumbhole. Photo courtesy of Remington Arms Co.

- **Model 700 SPS Varmint**—Features a synthetic stock with a vented beavertail fore-end, a 26" heavy contour barrel, and a trigger with adjustable pull weight. This model is offered in .17 Remington Fireball, .204 Ruger, .223 Remington, .22-250 Remington, .243 Winchester, and .308 Winchester.

Model 700 SPS Varmint. Photo courtesy of Remington Arms Co.

- **Model 700 Varmint SF**—Features a synthetic stock with a vented beavertail fore-end, a 26" heavy contour stainless fluted barrel, and a trigger with adjustable pull weight. This model is offered in .17 Remington Fireball, .204 Ruger, .223 Remington, .22-250 Remington, .220 Swift, and .308 Winchester.

Model 700 Varmint SF. Photo courtesy of Remington Arms Co.

- **Model 700 VTR**—Features a synthetic stock with a vented beavertail fore-end, a 22" triangular-contour barrel, and a trigger with adjustable pull weight. This model is offered in the following varmint cartridges: .204 Ruger, .223 Remington, .22-250 Remington, and .243 Winchester.

Model 700 VTR. Photo courtesy of Remington Arms Co.

- **Model Seven Predator**—Features a synthetic stock with a Mossy Oak Brush camo finish, a 22" fluted magnum-contour barrel, and the Remington X-Mark Pro trigger system. This model is offered in .17 Remington Fireball, .204 Ruger, .223 Remington, .22-250 Remington, and .243 Winchester.

Model Seven Predator. Photo courtesy of Remington Arms Co.

Ruger Firearms

William B. Ruger took a gamble in the 1960s, when other firearms makers were trending toward the Weatherby look, away from the traditional bolt-action style. He introduced the Model 77 bolt-action rifle in 1968, appealing to conservative riflemen. It had a traditional-looking walnut stock featuring an oil finish and hand checkering. Even though it retained many of the original Mauser features, the Model 77 was a truly modernized version of the 98 Mauser.

Even before the Model 77, in 1967 Bill Ruger offered a single-shot center-fire rifle based on the falling block action of the previous century. His design retained the classic looks of the British Farquharson action, but internally it was modern. While he is no longer with us, Bill Ruger's legacy lives on in the Model 77 bolt-action and No. 1 single-shot rifles.

For someone seeking a varmint rifle in the Ruger line, the selections include:

- **Model 77 Mark II Target**—Features a matte stainless-steel barreled action, a heavy contour 26" hammer-forged barrel (the 6.5 Creedmoor barrel is 28"), a target-style laminated stock with a wide fore-end, and a two-stage trigger with a light-pull, no-creep second stage. All Model 77s come standard with integral scope bases and 1" scope rings. Calibers offered for this model include the .204 Ruger, .223 Remington, .22-250 Remington, .243 Winchester, .25-06 Remington, 6.5 Creedmoor, and .308 Winchester.

Model 77 Mark II Target. Photo courtesy of Sturm, Ruger & Co., Inc.

- **Model 77 Hawkeye Standard**—Features the Model 77 action with integral scope mounts, a hammer-forged 22" or 24" sporter-weight barrel depending on the caliber, and the Ruger LC6 trigger. The Standard model has a classic hand-checkered walnut stock. Varmint calibers include the .204 Ruger, .223 Remington, .22-250 Remington, .243 Winchester, and .257 Roberts.

Model 77 Hawkeye Standard. Photo courtesy of Sturm, Ruger & Co., Inc.

- **Model 77 Hawkeye Predator**—This is a lightweight varmint rifle that features a 24" matte stainless-steel barreled action (22" in the .223 Remington) with integral scope mounts and the same two-stage trigger as the Mark II Target. The Predator model has a Green Mountain laminated stock. Calibers include the .204 Ruger, .223 Remington, and .22-250 Remington.

Model 77 Hawkeye Predator. Photo courtesy of Sturm, Ruger & Co., Inc.

- **No. 1 Varminter**—This is a classic single-shot rifle featuring a heavyweight 24" hammer-forged barrel, a two-piece hand-checkered walnut stock with a wide fore-end, and scope mounting blocks. Calibers include the .223 Remington, .22-250 Remington, .25-06 Remington, and 6.5 Creedmoor.

No. 1 Varminter. Photo courtesy of Sturm, Ruger & Co., Inc.

Sako

Established in 1921 and based in Finland, Sako has been producing high-quality sporting rifles for decades. Its latest bolt action, the Model 85 Series, offers two rifles designed specifically for the varmint shooter.

- **Model 85 Varmint**—Features a walnut stock with a wide forearm, a $23\frac{5}{8}$" free-floating hammer-forged heavy barrel, and an adjustable single-set trigger. It's offered in two action lengths. The XS action is chambered for the .204 Ruger, .222 Remington, and .223 Remington. The longer S action is chambered for the .22-250 Remington and .243 Winchester.

Model 85 Varmint. Photo courtesy of Sako Limited.

- **Model 85 Varmint Laminated Stainless**—Features a laminated stock with a wide fore-arm, a 23⅝" free-floating hammer-forged fluted heavy barrel, and an adjustable single-set trigger. It's offered in two action lengths.

The XS action is chambered for the .204 Ruger, .222 Remington, and .223 Remington. The longer S action is chambered for the .22-250 Remington and .243 Winchester.

Model 85 Varmint Laminated Stainless. Photo courtesy of Sako Limited.

Savage Arms

In 1956, Savage introduced a new bolt-action center-fire rifle—the Model 110. This rifle was designed to be manufactured economically without sacrificing anything in performance when compared with its competitors. The Model 110 has proven to be accurate, and recently the trigger was upgraded to the Savage AccuTrigger. Many variations of the original Model 110 are now offered, including the Model 12 Varmint Series, which should appeal to anyone looking for an accurate varmint rifle. The Model 12 Varmint Series includes the following.

- **Model 12 BTCSS**—Features a 26" fluted stainless-steel barrel, a laminated thumb-hole stock with a wide ventilated fore-end, and the Savage AccuTrigger. Calibers include the .204 Ruger, .223 Remington, and .22-250 Remington.

Varmint Series Model 12 BTCSS. Photo courtesy of Savage Arms.

- **Model 12 BVSS**—Features a 26" fluted stainless-steel barrel, a laminated target-style stock, and the Savage AccuTrigger.

Varmint calibers include the .223 Remington and .22-250 Remington.

Varmint Series Model 12 BVSS. Photo courtesy of Savage Arms.

- **Model 12 VLP DBM**—Features a 26" fluted stainless-steel barrel, a laminated target-style stock with a wide fore-end, a detachable magazine, and the Savage AccuTrigger. Varmint calibers include the .204 Ruger, .223 Remington, and .22-250 Remington.

Varmint Series Model 12 VLP DBM. Photo courtesy of Savage Arms.

- **Model 12 FCV**—Features a 26" carbon steel barrel, the Savage synthetic AccuStock, and the Savage AccuTrigger. Calibers include the .204 Ruger, .223 Remington, and .22-250 Remington. The Model 12 FLV is similar to the Model 12 FCV, except it features a left-handed action.

Varmint Series Model 12 FCV. Photo courtesy of Savage Arms.

- **Model 12 FV**—Features a 26" carbon steel barrel, a synthetic stock, and the Savage AccuTrigger. Calibers include the .204 Ruger, .223 Remington, and .22-250 Remington.

Varmint Series Model 12 FV. Photo courtesy of Savage Arms.

In addition to the Model 12 Varmint Series, Savage offers the following varmint rifles.

- **Model 14/114 American Classic**—This model features a 22" high-luster carbon steel barrel, an American walnut stock, and the Savage AccuTrigger. Calibers include the .223 Remington, .22-250 Remington, .243 Winchester, and .250 Savage.

Model 14/114 American Classic. Photo courtesy of Savage Arms.

- **Model 25 Lightweight Varminter-T**—This model features a laminated thumbhole stock with a ventilated fore-end, a 24" carbon steel barrel, a detachable box magazine, and the Savage AccuTrigger. Calibers include the .17 Hornet, .204 Ruger, .22 Hornet, .222 Remington, and .223 Remington.

Model 25 Lightweight Varminter-T. Photo courtesy of Savage Arms.

- **Model 25 Walking Varminter**—The Model 25 Walking Varminter features a synthetic stock, a 22" carbon steel barrel, a detachable box magazine, and the Savage AccuTrigger. Calibers include the .17 Hornet, .204 Ruger, .22 Hornet, .222 Remington, and .223 Remington.

Model 25 Walking Varminter. Photo courtesy of Savage Arms.

- **Model 25 Lightweight Varminter**—The Model 25 Lightweight Varminter features a laminated stock, a 24" carbon steel barrel, a detachable box magazine, and the Savage AccuTrigger. Calibers include the .17 Hornet, .204 Ruger, .22 Hornet, and .223 Remington.

Model 25 Lightweight Varminter. Photo courtesy of Savage Arms.

Tikka

Tikka rifles are manufactured in Finland by Sako. The Model T3 Series offers accurate rifles at a more moderate price than their Sako brethren. Tikka T3 varmint rifles include the following.

- **Model T3 Varmint**—Features a synthetic stock with a wide forearm that is adjustable for length of pull by adding spacers to the butt plate, a 23¾" free-floating hammer-forged heavy barrel, an adjustable single-stage trigger (set trigger is optional), and a box magazine. The T3 Varmint is available in the following varmint calibers: .204 Ruger, .222 Remington, .223 Remington, .22-250 Remington, and .243 Winchester.

Model T3 Varmint. Photo courtesy of Sako Limited.

- **Model T3 Varmint Stainless**—Features a synthetic stock with a wide forearm that is adjustable for length of pull by adding spacers to the butt plate, a stainless-steel action, a 23¾" free-floating, hammer-forged heavy barrel, an adjustable single-stage trigger (set trigger is optional), and a box magazine. The T3 Varmint Stainless is available in the following varmint calibers: .204 Ruger, .222 Remington, .223 Remington, .22-250 Remington, and .243 Winchester.

Model T3 Varmint Stainless. Photo courtesy of Sako Limited.

- **Model T3 Super Varmint**—Features a synthetic stock with a wide forearm that is adjustable for length of pull by adding spacers to the butt plate, an adjustable cheek piece, a stainless-steel action, a 23¾" free-floating hammer-forged heavy barrel, an adjustable single-stage trigger (set trigger is optional), a Picatinny rail, and a box magazine. The T3 Super Varmint is available in the following varmint calibers: .204 Ruger, .222 Remington, .223 Remington, .22-250 Remington, and .243 Winchester.

Model T3 Super Varmint. Photo courtesy of Sako Limited.

Weatherby Rifles

In 1945, Roy Weatherby founded a company in Southern California that allowed him to implement his ideas about cartridges using lightweight bullets at a high velocity and to subsequently design an action that could safely handle these Weatherby Magnums, the Mark V. In 1970, Roy introduced the Vanguard action, which resulted in competitively priced rifles chambered for conventional cartridges. The following is included in the Vanguard Series.

- **Vanguard Series 2 Varmint Special**— Features the Weatherby Vanguard action, a lightweight composite stock with fore-end inserts and a right-side palm swell, a 22" No. 3 contour barrel, and a match-quality adjustable two-stage trigger. The Varmint Special is available in the following varmint calibers: .223 Remington and .22-250 Remington.

Vanguard Series 2 Varmint Special. Photo courtesy of Weatherby, Inc.

Winchester Repeating Arms

Winchester's Model 70 bolt-action rifle was introduced in 1937. This model was an upgraded version of the earlier Winchester Model 54. Over the years, the Model 70 has undergone some design changes, and in 2006 the New Haven, Connecticut, plant ceased manufacturing altogether. Today, however, the Model 70s being built in Columbia, South Carolina, are better than ever and continue to carry on the reputation of being "the Rifleman's Rifle." Model 70 varmint rifle choices include:

- **Model 70 Coyote Light**—Features a 24" medium-heavy fluted stainless barrel mounted into a skeletonized aluminum bedding block, a carbon fiber/fiberglass composite Bell and Carlson stock with flow-through vents on the fore-end, and Winchester's M.O.A. trigger. The varmint calibers available for this rifle are the .22-250 Remington and .243 Winchester.

Model 70 Coyote Light. Photo courtesy of Winchester Repeating Arms.

- **Model 70 Featherweight**—Features a 22" sporter barrel, an American walnut stock, and Winchester's M.O.A. trigger. The varmint calibers available for this rifle are the .22-250 Remington and the .243 Winchester.

The Model 70 Featherweight should definitely be considered by anyone looking for a walking-around varmint rifle or, for that matter, a dual varmint and medium-game rifle.

Model 70 Featherweight. Photo courtesy of Winchester Repeating Arms.

A number of smaller firearms companies produce what I consider semi-custom rifles. These manufacturers include Brown Precision, Cooper Firearms, Dakota Arms, and Nosler. Cooper Arms offers a variety of extremely accurate varmint rifles in both single-shot and repeating bolt actions and a variety of varmint calibers, including many wildcats. Dakota Arms builds the excellent Varminter, which is offered in standard, heavy-barreled, and heavy all-weather versions. Nosler includes the Model 48 Custom Varmint in its rifle lineup. On average, these rifles are more expensive than the varmint rifles offered by the major manufacturers.

Being somewhat conservative in my rifle tastes, I have only included what might be called traditional varmint rifles in this book. I realize there are a number of semiautomatic rifles, often referred to as black rifles, now available that equal the accuracy of their bolt-action cousins. However, I leave this type of "varmint" rifle to be addressed in someone else's book.

Also, most manufacturers chamber their standard sporter-style rifles in many of the varmint calibers. Often, these rifles are capable of accuracy comparable to their heavy-barreled brethren. For those who prefer a walking-around varmint rifle, the lighter-weight sporters are just the ticket.

All of the rifle manufacturers have websites where you can view the varmint rifles and calibers they offer. Next, you can pay a visit to your favorite gun shop and from there on you're on your own. Good luck!

VARMINT CARTRIDGES

It's easy to discern from the current factory rifle chamberings which varmint cartridges are most popular today. I consider the .223 Remington to be at the top of the heap, closely followed by the .22-250 Remington and .204 Ruger. The current factory listings in ascending order are .17 Hornet, .17 Remington Fireball, .22 Hornet, .204 Ruger, .222 Remington, .223 Remington, .22-250 Remington, .220 Swift, .243 Winchester, .250 Savage, and .257 Roberts. While a number of varmint rifles are also chambered for cartridges such as the .25-06 Remington, 6.5 Creedmore, .308 Winchester, and .300 Winchester Short Magnum (WSM), I consider these to be better suited for big-game hunting than for popping away at varmints.

Some cartridges have fallen by the wayside in recent times. They include the .17 Remington, .222 Remington Magnum, .223 Winchester Super Short Magnum (WSSM), .225 Winchester, .243 WSSM, and .25 WSSM. Following is a list of factory varmint cartridges, both current and discontinued, with a brief description of each.

- **.17 Hornet**—Recently developed by Hornady, this is the .22 Hornet necked down to

.17 caliber. It launches a 20-grain Hornady V-MAX bullet at a velocity of 3650 feet per second (fps). This cartridge is chambered in the Savage Model 25 Walking Varminter.

- **.17 Remington Fireball**—Released in 2008, this is Remington's answer to both the .17 Mach IV and its own .17 Remington. It's a version of the .221 Fireball necked down to .17 caliber. The advertised muzzle velocity of the .17 Fireball is 4000 fps for the 20-grain bullet and 3850 for the 25-grain bullet.

- **.17 Remington**—Introduced by Remington in 1971 and chambered in the Model 700 rifle, this cartridge was the result of necking the .223 Remington down to .17 caliber and moving the shoulder back .087". Because of its tendency to quickly foul barrels and its sensitivity to slight variations in powder charges, this cartridge did not become popular among varmint shooters.

- **.204 Ruger**—This cartridge was a joint venture between Ruger and Hornady in 2004 and is based on the .222 Remington Magnum. It has proven a popular varmint cartridge, especially with prairie dog shooters. Its light recoil and stretched-string trajectory make it ideal for such shooting.

- **.22 Hornet**—This cartridge has the distinction of being the oldest of the factory cartridges designed for varmint shooting that's still hanging in there today. Its basic design results from work done by Colonel Townsend Whelen and Captain G. L. Watkins at the Springfield Armory in the 1920s. The .22 Hornet is a great cartridge for shooting small varmints, such as prairie dogs and woodchucks, when the range is fewer than 200 yards. The Hornet should also be considered if your varmint shooting will be conducted near settled areas.

- **.221 Remington Fireball**—This cartridge was originally developed by Remington in 1962 for its bolt-action, single-shot handgun, the Remington XP-100. Chamber it in a rifle with a much longer barrel, and you can achieve velocities exceeding 3000 fps. Like the .22 Hornet, this is a great cartridge for use in settled areas. The effective range of the .221 Fireball exceeds that of the Hornet, though, by about 50 yards. This is a good varmint cartridge, especially when chambered in a rifle.

- **.222 Remington**—This cartridge was developed by Mike Walker of Remington in 1950. While no longer as popular as it was a few years ago, it has sired a number of cartridges based on its case. These include the .17 Fireball, .204 Ruger, .221 Fireball, .223 Remington, and .222 Remington Magnum. From the time of its release up until the mid-1970s, the triple deuce was one of the most popular cartridges of the benchrest fraternity. It was knocked off the throne by the .22 PPC and 6mm PPC. Regardless, this is still a fine little varmint cartridge.

- **.223 Remington**—This cartridge was sired by the .222 Remington, though its case is longer by 0.06". The .223 Remington is the result of research and development for a new military cartridge to replace the 7.62 NATO round in a lighter rifle. The military version, released in 1957, is known as the 5.56×45mm and was first chambered in the M16. It found extensive use in Vietnam. The .223 Remington is an accurate varmint cartridge and is probably the most popular factory varmint cartridge available today.

- **.222 Remington Magnum**—This cartridge was an experimental design, like its brother the .223 Remington, and for a time it competed as the cartridge to be chosen by the military. In the end, however, the .223 Remington won out. The case is 0.09" longer than the .223 Remington, so it holds slightly more powder. The fact that the .223 Remington was chosen by the military ensured that it would become more popular than the .222 Remington Magnum.

- **.225 Winchester**—When Winchester redesigned the Model 70 in 1964, it retired the excellent .220 Swift and replaced it with the .225 Winchester, a semi-rimmed cartridge based on the wildcat .219 Donaldson Wasp.

This cartridge never became popular, and its fate was sealed a year later when Remington legitimized the .22-250.

- **.22-250 Remington**—In 1965, Remington released this cartridge in its Model 700 rifle. The original cartridge began life in the 1930s as a wildcat based on necking the .250-3000 Savage down to .22 caliber. Its most popular version as a wildcat was probably the .22 Varminter by J. E. Gebby, who even had the name "Varminter" copyrighted. Remington made a wise move by legitimizing this wildcat. It is still one of the most popular varmint cartridges today—second only to the .223 Remington. The practical range of the .22-250 Remington exceeds 300 yards.

- **.220 Swift**—This is still the king of varmint cartridges even though its popularity has waned somewhat. You can pretty much thank Remington for keeping it alive today. When it was first introduced by Winchester in 1935 in the Model 54 bolt action, Winchester claimed a muzzle velocity of more than 4000 fps with a 46-grain bullet. In the beginning, reloaders all loaded the Swift hot to obtain this velocity and then started to complain of throat erosion and short barrel life. Winchester took steps, however, to correct this by switching to a stainless-steel barrel. Once Remington came out with the .22-250, the Swift began to decline in popularity; for a time no factory rifles were chambered for it. Ruger decided to chamber it in both the Model 77V and No. 1V for a brief period in the 1970s.

- **.223 WSSM**—After Winchester's success with a number of short magnums, it released a family of even shorter cartridges, one of which is the .223 WSSM, introduced in 2003. This cartridge gained a reputation as being hard on barrels; to my knowledge, it was only chambered in Winchester and Browning rifles. Also, the short, fat case body was difficult to feed from a staggered bolt-action magazine. It did not gain much popularity with varmint shooters, despite its impressive velocities. When Winchester recently came out with its new Model 70,

the company did not chamber any new rifles for this cartridge.

- **.243 Winchester**—This combination varmint and medium-game cartridge was designed by Winchester in 1955. It's based on necking the .308 Winchester down to .243, or 6mm, caliber. This became a popular dual-purpose round. With light 60- to 75-grain bullets, it's an excellent varmint cartridge. With heavier 100- to 105-grain bullets it's a great cartridge for medium-size game, such as whitetail deer and antelope. This cartridge remains popular today and is chambered by just about every firearms manufacturer.

- **6mm Remington**—The 6mm Remington is the standard 7×57mm Mauser cartridge necked down to 6mm. This is as good a cartridge as the .243 Winchester—maybe even better—but when Remington first released it in 1955 as the .244 Remington (the same year Winchester released the .243), it was viewed more as a varmint cartridge and used a twist of 1:12" to favor the lighter and shorter bullets. (Winchester used a twist of 1:10" for the .243.) Eventually, Remington changed the twist to 1:9" and renamed the cartridge the 6mm Remington. For whatever reason, the 6mm Remington never gained as much popularity as the .243 Winchester. Even though it can be loaded to slightly higher velocities, it isn't currently chambered in any factory rifle.

- **.243 WSSM**—Around the same time that Winchester came out with the .223 WSSM, it also debuted the .243 WSSM. This used the same case as the .223 WSSM, but had a neck size of .243. This cartridge succumbed to the same fate as its smaller-caliber brother, the .223 WSSM.

- **.250-3000 Savage**—This cartridge was designed for Savage by Charles Newton in 1915 to fit the Savage Model 99 lever-action rifle. Savage loaded it with an 87-grain bullet to achieve a muzzle velocity of 3000 fps—hence its name. This was, and still is, a good dual-purpose varmint and medium-game cartridge. But, like the .257

Roberts, it was pushed to near obsolescence by the .243 Winchester and .244 Remington in 1955. Recently, Savage has resurrected it as the .250 Savage in its Model 14/114 American Classic bolt-action rifle.

- **.257 Roberts**—The .257 Roberts is based on a design by Ned Roberts in which he necked the standard 7 × 57mm Mauser cartridge down to .25 caliber. With slight modifications to the shoulder angle, Remington made this a factory cartridge in 1934. Like the .250-3000 Savage, the .257 Roberts is a dual varmint and medium-game round. It has a slightly larger capacity than the .250-3000 Savage, which added a few 100 fps over the former. Also, like the .250-3000 Savage, the .257 Roberts was, and still is, a fine dual-purpose cartridge that was knocked off the pedestal by the 6mms.

- **.25 WSSM**—Everything that was said about the .223 and .243 WSSMs can be stated about this cartridge, as well. It used the same short case as the other two and pretty much suffered the same fate.

- **.25-06 Remington**—This was another cartridge that started life as a popular wildcat, designed by A. O. Niedner in 1920, and was then legitimized by Remington in 1969. The .25-06 could be considered the king of the dual-purpose cartridges. It will perform quite satisfactorily on varmints out to 400 yards with 75-grain bullets and will serve as a potent game rifle on deer- and antelope-size game when using 100- to 120-grain bullets. The only problem with using this cartridge on varmints is that its big bang may not go over well in settled areas. Because of its heavy recoil, this is not a round to consider for prairie dogs where numerous shots are afforded.

Some of the varmint rifles I have listed are also chambered for cartridges that I do not consider suitable as varmint cartridges. The following cartridges are more appropriate for use in big-bore competition and for big-game hunting.

- **6.5 Creedmoor**—This is a new cartridge design released by Hornady in 2008. It is basically the .308 Winchester necked down to .264 caliber. This cartridge is primarily designed as an "across the course" big-bore competition round and is not what I would consider a varmint cartridge. It is, however, now chambered by some manufacturers in their varmint rifles. Bullets of 95 to 100 grains can be loaded to a muzzle velocity of more than 3000 fps. Like the .25-06 Remington, it's not a cartridge I would advise using in settled areas.

- **.308 Winchester**—The .308 Winchester is the civilian version of the 7.62 × 51mm NATO cartridge and was released commercially in 1952, two years before the NATO version. This cartridge is about $\frac{1}{2}$" shorter than the .30-06, but only 10 percent shy in ballistic performance. The .308 Winchester is inherently accurate and, as a general rule, not finicky when it comes to handloading. Like the 6.5 Creedmore, this is not a cartridge I recommend using for varmint shooting.

- **.300 WSM**—As with the 6.5 Creedmore and .308 Winchester, I don't recommend using this as a varmint cartridge.

MY VARMINT RIFLES AND CARTRIDGES

The following chapters describe the varmint rifles that I have acquired over the years, starting in the mid-1950s, and the cartridges for which they are chambered. I have years of experience in handloading these cartridges and in shooting these rifles, some at woodchucks and all at the rifle range.

In each chapter, I provide some background information about the cartridge, describe my rifle/scope combination, list the currently available factory ammunition for that cartridge, and provide trajectory tables for the cartridge.

In the "Handloading" section of each chapter, I list some loads from the current reloading manuals based on what I consider good combinations of powder and bullets to produce the best loads for that cartridge. These are my choices, but you are certainly welcome to select other combinations you believe might produce better results in your rifle. You may have already obtained satisfactory results with a powder I have not included in the tables, or you may decide to try a different powder than what I've listed.

In the load tables for each cartridge, I have listed the minimum and maximum powder charges. For developing a load, I recommend you pick a powder charge comfortably below the maximum listed. If you obtain good results with regard to both accuracy and velocity, and are safely below the maximum charge, then in my opinion you have developed a good varmint load for your rifle.

In the "Range Tests" section of each chapter, I evaluate both a factory and a handload version of that cartridge. All testing was done at 100 yards from a benchrest using a pedestal with front and rear sandbags. The velocities were measured at approximately 10 feet from the muzzle using an Oehler Model 35P chronograph.

I did not perform extensive testing of each cartridge. For the evaluation, I fired two groups, five shots each, of both a representative factory cartridge and my handload. Regard this as a sampling that might indicate what the rifle/cartridge combination is capable of. If you don't reload, you should experiment with different brands of factory ammo and bullet weights to determine what works best for your rifle.

Chapter 2
.204 Ruger

The .204 Ruger, introduced in 2004, is currently one of the most popular cartridges for the varmint shooting crowd. This cartridge is chambered in a variety of rifles by almost all of the major rifle manufacturers. The .204 Ruger is the result of a joint development effort between Hornady and Ruger. Basically, it's the .222 Remington Magnum case necked down to .20 caliber with minimal body taper and a sharp 30 degree shoulder. Hornady factory loads for the 32-grain V-MAX bullet exceed a muzzle velocity of 4200 fps.

This cartridge has negligible recoil and is pleasant to shoot from the benchrest or in the field, especially when prairie dogs result in prolonged shooting. The .204 Ruger should also be considered if you plan to hunt varmints in settled neighborhoods.

THE CZ MODEL 527 AMERICAN

The CZ Model 527 is a direct descendant of the Czech Brno Model ZB miniature Mauser action rifle that was imported into the United States for a brief period following World War II. That rifle was chambered for the popular .22 Hornet. When the Iron Curtain fell on Czechoslovakia, the little rifle was no longer available in the United States. After the breakup of the Soviet Union, however, the new Czech Republic was once again able to offer fine rifles to American shooters. In 1997, CZ-USA, located in Kansas City, Kansas, became the sole distributor for CZ firearms in the United States.

The Model 527 is a modern version of the miniature Mauser action, and includes integral scope mounting bases. The Model 527 American features a nicely figured Turkish walnut stock, a 21.9" free-floating hammer-forged sporter-weight barrel, a five-round detachable magazine, an adjustable single-set trigger, and 1" steel scope rings. The rifling twist for the .204 Ruger is 1:12".

The unset trigger pull was adjusted to three pounds and the set pull to one pound. In both cases, the trigger has no creep and breaks cleanly.

The scope is a Nikon Monarch 3-9×40mm variable that features Nikon's Bullet Drop Compensator (BDC) reticle. With its light weight of about seven pounds with scope and mounts and its short, sporter contour barrel, I consider the Model 527 American a great walking-around varmint rifle.

Author's CZ 527 American—.204 Ruger.

.204 RUGER FACTORY AMMO

Factory ammunition for the .204 Ruger is available from Federal, Hornady, Nosler, Remington, and Winchester.

With its high velocity and flat trajectory, I believe this cartridge is suitable for varmints, such as prairie dogs and woodchucks, out to 350 yards or more.

The .204 Ruger, released in 2004, is the result of a joint development project between Hornady and Ruger.

This cartridge is basically the .222 Remington Magnum necked down to .20 caliber. The Hornady 32-grain factory load produces a muzzle velocity of 4225 fps.

Federal Premium Ammunition

Bullet Weight (Grains)	Bullet Type	Velocity (fps)					Energy (ft-lbs)				
		Muzzle	100 yards	200 yards	300 yards	400 yards	Muzzle	100 yards	200 yards	300 yards	400 yards
32	Speer TNT Green	4030	3316	2706	2172	1705	1154	781	520	335	207
32	Nosler Ballistic Tip	4030	3465	2968	2523	2119	1154	853	626	452	319
40	Nosler Ballistic Tip	3650	3200	2793	2421	2079	1183	909	693	520	384

Hornady Varmint Express Ammunition

Bullet Weight (Grains)	Bullet Type	Velocity (fps)					Energy (ft-lbs)				
		Muzzle	100 yards	200 yards	300 yards	400 yards	Muzzle	100 yards	200 yards	300 yards	400 yards
24	NTX	4400	3668	3045	2502	2020	1032	717	494	334	217
32	V-MAX	4225	3645	3137	2683	2272	1268	944	699	512	367
40	V-MAX	3900	3482	3103	2755	2433	1351	1077	855	674	526
45	SP	3625	3188	2792	2428	2093	1313	1015	788	589	438

Nosler Trophy Grade Varmint Ammunition

Bullet Weight (Grains)	Bullet Type	Velocity (fps)					Energy (ft-lbs)				
		Muzzle	100 yards	200 yards	300 yards	400 yards	Muzzle	100 yards	200 yards	300 yards	400 yards
32	BTLF	3800	3319	2890	2499	2140	1026	783	593	444	325

Nosler Varmageddon Ammunition

Bullet Weight (Grains)	Bullet Type	Velocity (fps)					Energy (ft-lbs)				
		Muzzle	100 yards	200 yards	300 yards	400 yards	Muzzle	100 yards	200 yards	300 yards	400 yards
32	FBHP	4000	3148	2438	1832	1347	1137	704	422	239	129
32	FBSP	4000	3433	2934	2487	2081	1137	837	612	439	308

Remington AccuTip-V

Bullet Weight (Grains)	Bullet Type	Velocity (fps)					Energy (ft-lbs)				
		Muzzle	100 yards	200 yards	300 yards	400 yards	Muzzle	100 yards	200 yards	300 yards	400 yards
32	AccuTip-V	4225	3632	3114	2652	2234	1268	937	689	500	355
40	AccuTip-V	3900	3451	3046	2667	2336	1351	1058	824	636	485

Winchester Varmint Ammunition

Bullet Weight (Grains)	Bullet Type	Velocity (fps)					Energy (ft-lbs)				
		Muzzle	100 yards	200 yards	300 yards	400 yards	Muzzle	100 yards	200 yards	300 yards	400 yards
32	Ballistic Silvertip	4050	3482	2984	2537	2132	1165	862	632	457	323
34	Super-X HP	4025	3339	2751	2232	1775	1223	842	571	376	238

HANDLOADING THE .204 RUGER

Of the current crop of reloading manuals, only Hornady, Lyman, and Nosler list reloading data for the .204 Ruger. In addition to these manuals, Hodgdon publishes an annual reloading manual in magazine format that includes .204 Ruger load data.

Hornady Handbook of Cartridge Reloading, 8th Edition

In examining the load tables for the .204 Ruger in the *Hornady Handbook of Cartridge Reloading*, 8th edition, you will find loads listed for the 32- and 40-grain V-MAX bullets, as well as the 45-grain SP bullet. According to Hornady, the .204 Ruger likes powders with a medium burn rate, such as RL 15, Benchmark, H4895, IMR 4064, and W748. The highest muzzle velocity achieved with the 32-grain V-MAX bullet was 4200 fps with 29.2 grains of Vihtavuori N140 powder. This was a maximum charge. Accurate 2520 and Winchester 748, which are both ball powders, provided the highest velocity, 3850 fps, with the 40-grain V-MAX bullet. Reloder 15, Varget, and W 748 all produced the highest velocities with the 45-grain bullet. Hornady did not identify which loads were the most accurate.

Lyman Reloading Handbook, 49th Edition

Referring to the *Lyman Reloading Handbook*, 49th edition, the most accurate load for the 32-grain bullet was 23.7 grains of Vihtavuori N130. This charge, which was the maximum, produced a muzzle velocity of 3871 fps. Lyman's most accurate powder for the 40-grain bullet was H335, where a maximum charge of 26.6 grains gave a muzzle velocity of 3660 fps. Again, these loads were tested in a 24 inch barrel. Neither this powder nor H322 were even listed in the Hornady book.

The most accurate load tested with the 45-grain bullet was 24.2 grains of IMR 4895 powder, which produced a muzzle velocity of 3225 fps.

Nosler Reloading Guide No. 6

Nosler Reloading Guide No. 6 lists loads for the company's 32- and 40-grain Solid Base Ballistic Tip bullets. Nosler's most accurate load for the 32-grain bullet was 21 grains of IMR 4198. It shows that a maximum charge of 23 grains of this powder produced a muzzle velocity of 4060 fps in a 26 inch barrel. The most accurate

load tested for the Nosler 40-grain bullet was with 22.52 grains of Hodgdon H322 powder. A maximum charge of this powder, which is 24.5 grains, gave a muzzle velocity of 3608 fps.

Nosler obtained the highest muzzle velocity for the 40-grain bullet, which was 709 fps, with 28 grains of IMR 4895 powder. This was a maximum charge. Interestingly, Hornady achieved this same velocity with 26.2 grains of H4895, which is similar to, but not exactly the same as, the IMR powder. The IMR 4895 burning rate is slightly slower. Both the Hornady and Nosler manuals list Hodgdon's Benchmark powder for the 32- and 40-grain bullets.

Sierra 5th Edition Reloading Manual

Even though load data for the .204 Ruger is not listed in the current Sierra manual, you may contact the company and it will provide you with the load data. That is how I obtained the data listed below.

The following tables list load data from the current reloading manuals for some of the popular powders for .204 Ruger bullet weights of 32, 40, and 45 grains.

Hodgdon Benchmark Powder—32-Grain Bullet

Manual	Minimum Charge	Muzzle Velocity	Maximum Charge	Muzzle Velocity	Barrel Length, Twist Rate
Hornady	25.1 grains	3700 fps	28.0 grains	4100 fps	26" barrel, 1:12"
Lyman	25.9 grains	3671 fps	27.3 grains	3938 fps	24" barrel, 1:12"
Nosler	25.5 grains	3809 fps	27.5 grains	4110 fps	26" barrel, 1:12"
Sierra	26.0 grains	3700 fps	27.9 grains	4000 fps	26" barrel, 1:12"

Hodgdon Benchmark Powder—39/40-Grain Bullets

Manual	Minimum Charge	Muzzle Velocity	Maximum Charge	Muzzle Velocity	Barrel Length, Twist Rate
Hornady	23.6 grains	3400 fps	26.0 grains	3700 fps	26" barrel, 1:12"
Lyman	23.7 grains	3378 fps	25.0 grains	3615 fps	24" barrel, 1:12"
Nosler	24.0 grains	3374 fps	26.0 grains	3664 fps	26" barrel, 1:12"
Sierra	23.3 grains	3200 fps	25.7 grains	3600 fps	26" barrel, 1:12"

.204 Ruger

Hodgdon Benchmark Powder—45-Grain Bullet*

Manual	Minimum Charge	Muzzle Velocity	Maximum Charge	Muzzle Velocity	Barrel Length, Twist Rate
Lyman	22.8 grains	3236 fps	24.0 grains	3379 fps	24" barrel, 1:12"

*The Hornady manual does not list Benchmark powder for the 45-grain bullet. The Nosler manual does not list a 45-grain bullet for the .204 Ruger. Sierra does not provide data for a 45-grain bullet.

IMR 4895 Powder—32-Grain Bullet*

Manual	Minimum Charge	Muzzle Velocity	Maximum Charge	Muzzle Velocity	Barrel Length, Twist Rate
Hornady	25.9 grains	3700 fps	28.4 grains	4100 fps	26" barrel, 1:12"
Lyman	27.5 grains	3707 fps	29.0 grains	3986 fps	24" barrel, 1:12"
Nosler	27.0 grains	3819 fps	29.0 grains	4094 fps	26" barrel, 1:12"
Sierra	26.0 grains	3500 fps	28.3 grains	3950 fps	26" barrel, 1:12"

*The Hornady manual lists H4895 powder, which is similar to IMR 4895 powder but not identical in burning characteristics.

IMR 4895 Powder—39/40-Grain Bullets*

Manual	Minimum Charge	Muzzle Velocity	Maximum Charge	Muzzle Velocity	Barrel Length, Twist Rate
Hornady	24.5 grains	3400 fps	26.7 grains	3800 fps	26" barrel, 1:12"
Lyman	25.4 grains	3427 fps	26.8 grains	3660 fps	24" barrel, 1:12"
Nosler	26.0 grains	3445 fps	28.0 grains	3709 fps	26" barrel, 1:12"
Sierra	25.0 grains	3200 fps	27.5 grains	3700 fps	26" barrel, 1:12"

*The Hornady manual lists H4895 powder, which is similar to IMR 4895 powder but not identical in burning characteristics.

IMR 4895 Powder—45-Grain Bullet*

Manual	Minimum Charge	Muzzle Velocity	Maximum Charge	Muzzle Velocity	Barrel Length, Twist Rate
Hornady	21.1 grains	3100 fps	24.8 grains	3500 fps	26" barrel, 1:12"
Lyman	24.2 grains	3225 fps	25.5 grains	3441 fps	24" barrel, 1:12"

*The Hornady manual lists H4895 powder, which is similar to IMR 4895 powder but not identical in burning characteristics. The Nosler manual does not list a 45-grain bullet for the .204 Ruger. Sierra does not provide data for a 45-grain bullet.

Hodgdon H322 Powder—32-Grain Bullet*

Manual	Minimum Charge	Muzzle Velocity	Maximum Charge	Muzzle Velocity	Barrel Length, Twist Rate
Lyman	25.4 grains	3740 fps	26.7 grains	3911 fps	24" barrel, 1:12"
Nosler	24.5 grains	3825 fps	26.5 grains	4112 fps	26" barrel, 1:12"
Sierra	25.2 grains	3700 fps	26.2 grains	3900 fps	26" barrel, 1:12"

*The Hornady manual does not list H322 powder for the .204 Ruger.

Hodgdon H322 Powder—39/40-Grain Bullets*

Manual	Minimum Charge	Muzzle Velocity	Maximum Charge	Muzzle Velocity	Barrel Length, Twist Rate
Lyman	23.7 grains	3403 fps	25.0 grains	3567 fps	24" barrel, 1:12"
Nosler	22.5 grains	3340 fps	24.5 grains	3608 fps	26" barrel, 1:12"
Sierra	22.7 grains	3200 fps	24.2 grains	3500 fps	26" barrel, 1:12"

*The Hornady manual does not list H322 powder for the .204 Ruger.

Note: The Hornady and Lyman manuals do not list H322 powder for the 45-grain bullet. The Nosler manual does not list a 45-grain bullet for the .204 Ruger. Sierra does not provide data for a 45-grain bullet.

Hodgdon VARGET Powder—32-Grain Bullet

Manual	Minimum Charge	Muzzle Velocity	Maximum Charge	Muzzle Velocity	Barrel Length, Twist Rate
Hornady	27.0 grains	3700 fps	29.3 grains	4000 fps	26" barrel, 1:12"
Lyman	27.5 grains	3706 fps	29.0 grains	3897 fps	24" barrel, 1:12"
Nosler	27.0 grains	3811 fps	29.0 grains	4043 fps	26" barrel, 1:12"
Sierra	26.0 grains	3500 fps	28.8 grains	3900 fps	26" barrel, 1:12"

Hodgdon VARGET Powder—39/40-Grain Bullets

Manual	Minimum Charge	Muzzle Velocity	Maximum Charge	Muzzle Velocity	Barrel Length, Twist Rate
Hornady	25.2 grains	3400 fps	27.8 grains	3700 fps	26" barrel, 1:12"
Lyman	26.0 grains	3545 fps	27.4 grains	3653 fps	24" barrel, 1:12"
Nosler	25.5 grains	3407 fps	27.5 grains	3648 fps	26" barrel, 1:12"
Sierra	25.0 grains	3200 fps	28.0 grains	3700 fps	26" barrel, 1:12"

Hodgdon VARGET Powder—45-Grain Bullet*

Manual	Minimum Charge	Muzzle Velocity	Maximum Charge	Muzzle Velocity	Barrel Length, Twist Rate
Hornady	22.4 grains	3100 fps	26.7 grains	3600 fps	26" barrel, 1:12"
Lyman	23.8 grains	3246 fps	25.1 grains	3416 fps	24" barrel, 1:12"

*The Nosler manual does not list a 45-grain bullet for the .204 Ruger. Sierra does not provide data for a 45-grain bullet.

RANGE TESTS

The weather conditions were favorable on the day I performed the range testing of the .204 Ruger. There was a variable breeze from about 12 o'clock, the temperature was in the high 80s, and it was a bright, sunny day.

I used Hornady's 32-grain V-MAX ammo for the factory cartridge portion of the .204 Ruger range test. As can be seen from the test targets on the next page, this is reasonably accurate ammunition. For those of you who are not handloaders, I suggest you consider the Hornady factory ammunition, as well as the other brands mentioned earlier in this chapter.

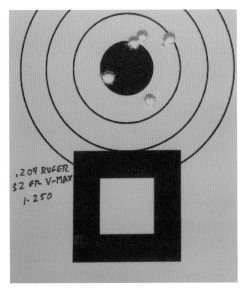

.204 Ruger—Factory Ammo Group 1.

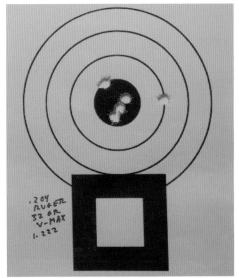

.204 Ruger—Factory Ammo Group 2.

Group 1 measured 1.25" center to center; group 2 measured 1.22" with four shots in 0.67".

The Oehler Model 35P chronograph printout indicates that only the first five shots registered on the second stop screen. I'm not sure why this occurred, but maybe it was the combination of high velocity, small bullet size, and the fact that there was bright sunlight. Anyway, I think the first five shots that did register are indicative of the Hornady V-MAX cartridge's velocity. The average velocity of 4045 fps compares favorably with the 4225 fps listed by Hornady when you consider that my rifle has a 21.9 inch barrel.

The handload—a Sierra 32-grain BlitzKing bullet, 26.5 grains of Hodgdon's Benchmark powder, Remington 7½ primer, and Hornady brass—produced the five-shot groups on the following page.

The first group measured 0.93" with four of the shots in 0.52". The second group measured 0.77" with four of the shots in 0.40". I consider this very good accuracy for a lightweight sporter, such as the CZ 527 American.

The chronograph registered all ten shots for the handloads and measured an average velocity of 3559 fps. This agrees with Sierra's published velocity of 3700 fps for 26 grains of Benchmark powder, considering that my rifle

```
2877-01-2875-
2863-02-2861-
2930-03-2926-
2871-04-2869-
2888-05-2886-
2960-06-2908-
---------
06-2926-+
06-2861--
06-0065-T
06-2887-M
06-0024-$
---------
```

The printout from the Oehler 35P chronograph for Hornady's 32-grain V-MAX factory ammo indicates an average velocity (M) of 4045 fps. A standard deviation ($) of 23 fps indicates a consistent load.

While Hornady lists a muzzle velocity of 4225 fps for this cartridge, the lower readings from my test can be attributed to the fact that my CZ 527 has a 21.9 inch barrel. It's possible that Hornady used a 26 inch barrel for its tests.

has a 21.9 inch barrel and Sierra's testing was done using a 26 inch barrel.

Since this load is approximately midway between the minimum and maximum charges for Benchmark powder listed in the reloading manuals, the pressure signs are good, and the accuracy is acceptable, I think I will stick with this load for now. Still, I might try some other powders in the future, such as Hodgdon's H322 and Varget.

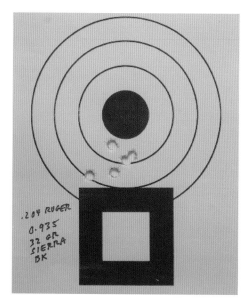

.204 Ruger—Handload Group 1.

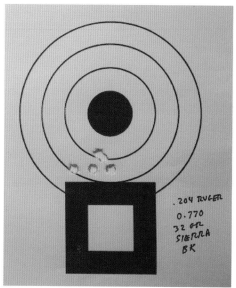

.204 Ruger—Handload Group 2.

```
3581-01-3568-
3490-02-3478-
3502-03-3491-
3571-04-3558-
3565-05-3557-
3587-06-3568-
3623-07-3601-
3616-08-3598-
3590-09-3573-
3623-10-3603-
----------
10-3603-+
10-3478--
10-0125-T
10-3559-M
10-0043-$
----------
```

For my handload, the Oehler 35P chronograph indicates an average velocity (M) of 3559 fps and a standard deviation ($) of 43 fps.

This average velocity reading agrees with that published by Sierra, considering its testing was performed with a 26 inch barrel.

TRAJECTORY TABLES

The following trajectory tables were developed using the Handloads.com ballistic calculator. The tables are based on the line of sight (LOS) being 1.5 inches above the line of fire (LOF). All tabular data is expressed in inches.

32-Grain Bullet (BC = .210)

Muzzle Velocity (fps)	Muzzle	100 yards	200 yards	300 yards	400 yards
	−1.5	0.0	−1.5	−7.0	−18.2
4000	−1.5	0.7	0.0	−4.8	−15.2
	−1.5	2.3	3.2	0.0	−8.8
	−1.5	0.0	−1.6	−7.6	−19.5
3900	−1.5	0.8	0.0	−5.1	−16.2
	−1.5	2.5	3.4	0.0	−9.4
	−1.5	0.0	−1.8	−8.2	−20.8
3800	−1.5	0.9	0.0	−5.4	−17.2
	−1.5	2.7	3.6	0.0	−9.9
	−1.5	0.0	−2.0	−8.8	−22.3
3700	−1.5	1.0	0.0	−5.8	−18.3
	−1.5	2.9	3.9	0.0	−10.6
	−1.5	0.0	−2.2	−9.5	−24.0
3600	−1.5	1.1	0.0	−6.2	−19.6
	−1.5	3.2	4.1	0.0	−11.3

39/40-Grain Bullets (BC = .275)

Muzzle Velocity (fps)	Muzzle	100 yards	200 yards	300 yards	400 yards
	−1.5	0.0	−1.6	−7.0	−17.4
3800	−1.5	0.8	0.0	−4.7	−14.3
	−1.5	2.3	3.1	0.0	−8.0
	−1.5	0.0	−1.7	−7.6	−18.7
3700	−1.5	0.9	0.0	−5.0	−15.2
	−1.5	2.5	3.3	0.0	−8.6
	−1.5	0.0	−1.9	−8.2	−20.6
3600	−1.5	1.0	0.0	−5.3	−16.1
	−1.5	2.7	3.5	0.0	−9.7
	−1.5	0.0	−2.1	−8.9	−21.6
3500	−1.5	1.1	0.0	−5.7	−17.3
	−1.5	3.0	3.8	0.0	−9.7
	−1.5	0.0	−2.4	−9.6	−23.2
3400	−1.5	1.2	0.0	−6.1	−18.5
	−1.5	3.2	4.1	0.0	−10.4

45-Grain Bullet (BC = .245)

Muzzle Velocity (fps)	Muzzle	100 yards	200 yards	300 yards	400 yards
	−1.5	0.0	−2.0	−8.7	−21.5
3600	−1.5	1.0	0.0	−5.6	−17.4
	−1.5	2.9	3.7	0.0	−9.9
	−1.5	0.0	−2.3	−9.4	−23.1
3500	−1.5	1.1	0.0	−6.0	−18.6
	−1.5	3.1	4.0	0.0	−10.6
	−1.5	0.0	−2.5	−10.2	−24.9
3400	−1.5	1.2	0.0	−6.5	−20.0
	−1.5	3.4	4.3	0.0	−11.3
	−1.5	0.0	−2.7	−11.1	−26.9
3300	−1.5	1.4	0.0	−7.0	−21.4
	−1.5	3.7	4.6	0.0	−12.1
	−1.5	0.0	−3.0	−12.0	−29.1
3200	−1.5	1.5	0.0	−7.5	−23.0
	−1.5	4.0	5.0	0.0	−13.1
	−1.5	0.0	−3.3	−13.1	−31.5
3100	−1.5	1.7	0.0	−8.1	−24.9
	−1.5	4.4	5.4	0.0	−14.1

Chapter 3

.221 Remington Fireball

The .221 Fireball was developed by Remington in 1963 for its XP-100 single-shot pistol. While Remington no longer makes the pistol, the .221 Fireball has continued to gain popularity as a rifle cartridge. It's a slightly shortened version of the famous .222 Remington cartridge. In a rifle barrel, the .221 Fireball can attain muzzle velocities of more than 3000 fps with 40-grain bullets.

Offering excellent accuracy and a mild report, this cartridge is ideally suited as a varmint cartridge for use in settled areas. Its effective range for woodchucks and prairie dogs is about 250 yards. With 55-grain bullets, the .221 Fireball is also a good coyote cartridge.

THE COOPER MODEL 21 VARMINTER

Cooper Firearms of Montana makes (maybe *creates* is a better word) a full line of high-quality rifles and offers many optional features. But even without any of the optional features, Cooper rifles should be considered semi-custom rifles. All these rifles are guaranteed to shoot $\frac{1}{2}''$ three-shot groups at 100 yards.

The Cooper Model 21 Varminter is a single-shot bolt-action rifle with a medium-heavy 24 inch stainless-steel free-floating barrel and an AA grade Claro walnut stock. This is the most popular style of the Cooper rifle lineup. The Model 21 Varminter, as a single-shot bolt action, does not require an opening at the bottom of the action or a cutout in the stock for a magazine. This results in a stiffer action, which is conducive to accuracy. Also, the stock features hand checkering and a hand-rubbed oil finish. To further enhance accuracy, the action is epoxy bedded in the stock at both the tang and recoil lug areas.

The rifling twist for the .221 Fireball is 1:12".

The trigger is fully adjustable, and I adjusted the pull on this rifle to one and a half pounds. There is no creep, and the trigger breaks cleanly.

The scope is a variable power 6-24×40mm Bushnell Elite 4200 with $\frac{1}{8}$ MOA windage and elevation adjustments. It has an adjustable objective for parallax correction. The scope is mounted in Leupold high rings.

This is a true varmint rifle. With its 24 inch medium-heavy barrel and wide forearm stock, the Model 21 Varminter, in combination with its scope and mounts, weighs close to nine pounds.

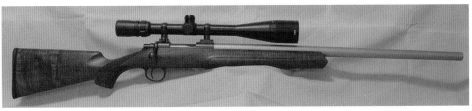

Author's Cooper Model 21 Varminter—.221 Remington Fireball.

.221 REMINGTON FIREBALL FACTORY AMMO

Factory ammunition for the .221 Remington Fireball is available from Nosler and Remington. You'll probably need to search online for a supplier. Unfortunately, this great little cartridge is not as popular as it should be.

With its moderately high velocity and flat trajectory, the .221 Fireball is suitable for varmints, such as prairie dogs and woodchucks, out to 250 yards. This cartridge is definitely a choice for varmint shooting in settled areas where noise could be a factor.

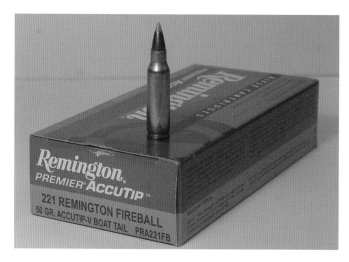

The .221 Remington Fireball is a great cartridge for varmint shooting in settled areas where noise may be a factor. It is deadly on prairie dogs and woodchucks at ranges up to 250 yards.

Nosler Varmageddon Ammunition

Bullet Weight (Grains)	Bullet Type	Velocity (fps)				Energy (ft-lbs)			
		Muzzle	100 yards	200 yards	300 yards	Muzzle	100 yards	200 yards	300 yards
40	FBHP	3100	2510	1991	1547	853	560	352	213
40	FPSP	3100	2651	2244	1874	853	624	447	312

Remington AccuTip-V Ammunition

Bullet Weight (Grains)	Bullet Type	Velocity (fps)				Energy (ft-lbs)			
		Muzzle	100 yards	200 yards	300 yards	Muzzle	100 yards	200 yards	300 yards
50	AccuTip-V	2995	2605	2247	1918	996	753	560	408

HANDLOADING THE .221 REMINGTON FIREBALL

In the case of the .221 Fireball, handloading is definitely a consideration. Handloaders will have much more flexibility when it comes to this cartridge. Bullet weights range from 40 to 55 grains. Only the Hornady, Nosler, and Sierra manuals, however, list rifle data for the .221 Fireball. Since this book is about varmint rifles, we will not consider handgun loads from the other manuals.

32

Hornady Handbook of Cartridge Reloading, 8th Edition

Hornady Handbook lists loads for the Hornady 35-, 40-, 50-, and 55-grain V-MAX bullets, as well as loads for the 45-grain Hornet and Bee bullets. All loads were tested in a Remington Model 700 Classic rifle with a 24 inch barrel. Hornady's most accurate loads were with the 50-grain V-MAX bullet and IMR 4198 powder. RL 7 yielded the highest velocities, which exceeded 3000 fps with the 50-grain bullet.

Nosler Reloading Guide No. 6

Loads for the .221 Fireball in the Nosler manual are listed for the Nosler 40-, 50-, 52-, and 55-grain bullets. They were tested using a rifle with a 22 inch barrel. For the 40-grain bullet, Nosler's most accurate powder was RL 7. For the 50- and 52-grain bullets, the most accurate powder was H4198. And for the 55-grain bullet, the most accurate powder was AA2015.

Sierra 5th Edition Reloading Manual

The Sierra manual includes loads for the Sierra 40-, 45-, 50-, 52-, 53-, and 55-grain bullets. The best accuracy was obtained using AA2015, Viht N130, H322, H4227, and RE-7 powders. AA2015 powder produced the best accuracy with the Sierra 40-grain bullets, and H322 powder produced the best accuracy with the Sierra 50-grain bullets.

The following tables list some loads from all three reloading manuals for the 40-, 45-, 50-, and 55-grain bullets. I consider these bullet weights to be a good match for the .221 Fireball when developing loads for varmint shooting for this cartridge.

Alliant Reloder 7 Powder—40-Grain Bullet*

Manual	Minimum Charge	Muzzle Velocity	Maximum Charge	Muzzle Velocity	Barrel Length, Twist Rate
Nosler	17.0 grains	2869 fps	19.0 grains	3242 fps	22" barrel, 1:14"
Sierra	17.2 grains	2600 fps	19.0 grains	3200 fps	20" barrel, 1:12"

*The Hornady manual does not list RL 7 powder for the 40-grain bullet.

Alliant Reloder 7 Powder—45-Grain Bullet*

Manual	Minimum Charge	Muzzle Velocity	Maximum Charge	Muzzle Velocity	Barrel Length, Twist Rate
Hornady	17.3 grains	2900 fps	19.5 grains	3300 fps	24" barrel, 1:12"
Sierra	16.7 grains	2600 fps	18.7 grains	3100 fps	20" barrel, 1:12"

*The Nosler manual does not list loads for the 45-grain bullet.

Alliant Reloder 7 Powder—50/52/53-Grain Bullets

Manual	Minimum Charge	Muzzle Velocity	Maximum Charge	Muzzle Velocity	Barrel Length, Twist Rate
Hornady	16.3 grains	2700 fps	18.6 grains	3100 fps	24" barrel, 1:12"
Nosler	16.0 grains	2594 fps	18.0 grains	2965 fps	22" barrel, 1:14"
Sierra	16.5 grains	2500 fps	18.6 grains	3000 fps	20" barrel, 1:12"

Alliant Reloder 7 Powder—55-Grain Bullet

Manual	Minimum Charge	Muzzle Velocity	Maximum Charge	Muzzle Velocity	Barrel Length, Twist Rate
Hornady	14.6 grains	2500 fps	17.7 grains	2900 fps	24" barrel, 1:12"
Nosler	15.5 grains	2483 fps	17.5 grains	2808 fps	22" barrel, 1:14"
Sierra	15.5 grains	2400 fps	17.5 grains	2800 fps	20" barrel, 1:12"

IMR 4198 Powder—40-Grain Bullet*

Manual	Minimum Charge	Muzzle Velocity	Maximum Charge	Muzzle Velocity	Barrel Length, Twist Rate
Hornady	15.8 grains	2900 fps	18.0 grains	3300 fps	24" barrel, 1:12"
Nosler	16.0 grains	2792 fps	18.0 grains	3259 fps	22" barrel, 1:14"
Sierra	16.0 grains	2600 fps	18.0 grains	3100 fps	20" barrel, 1:12"

*The Sierra manual lists H4198 powder, which is similar to IMR 4198 powder but not identical in burning characteristics.

IMR 4198 Powder—45-Grain Bullet*

Manual	Minimum Charge	Muzzle Velocity	Maximum Charge	Muzzle Velocity	Barrel Length, Twist Rate
Hornady	16.4 grains	2900 fps	17.4 grains	3100 fps	24" barrel, 1:12"
Sierra	15.9 grains	2600 fps	17.9 grains	3000 fps	20" barrel, 1:12"

*The Nosler manual does not list loads for the 45-grain bullet. The Sierra manual lists H4198 powder, which is similar to IMR 4198 powder but not identical in burning characteristics.

IMR 4198 Powder—50/52/53-Grain Bullets*

Manual	Minimum Charge	Muzzle Velocity	Maximum Charge	Muzzle Velocity	Barrel Length, Twist Rate
Hornady	14.8 grains	2600 fps	16.6 grains	2900 fps	24" barrel, 1:12"
Nosler	15.0 grains	2672 fps	17.0 grains	3034 fps	22" barrel, 1:14"
Sierra	15.7 grains	2500 fps	17.7 grains	2900 fps	20" barrel, 1:12"

*The Sierra manual lists H4198 powder, which is similar to IMR 4198 powder but not identical in burning characteristics.

IMR 4198 Powder—55-Grain Bullet*

Manual	Minimum Charge	Muzzle Velocity	Maximum Charge	Muzzle Velocity	Barrel Length, Twist Rate
Hornady	14.0 grains	2500 fps	15.8 grains	2700 fps	24" barrel, 1:12"
Nosler	15.0 grains	2547 fps	17.0 grains	2900 fps	22" barrel, 1:14"
Sierra	15.0 grains	2400 fps	17.4 grains	2800 fps	20" barrel, 1:12"

*The Sierra manual lists H4198 powder, which is similar to IMR 4198 powder but not identical in burning characteristics.

One powder that is only listed in the Hornady manual—and even then, only for the 35-grain bullet—is Hodgdon's Lil'Gun. In *Hodgdon's 2012 Annual Manual*, this powder is listed for all of the .221 Fireball bullet weights. I believe that regardless of the bullet weight, Lil'Gun should be considered by anyone planning on developing loads for the .221 Fireball.

Also, Hodgdon's H322 powder is only listed in the Sierra manual for the 50-, 52/53-, and

55-grain Sierra bullets—not for the 40- and 45-grain bullets. I think this powder should be considered for the 40- and 45-grain bullets, as well.

The following data for Hodgdon's Lil'Gun and H322 powder is from *Hodgdon's 2012 Manual.*

Hodgdon Lil'Gun and H322 Powder—40-Grain Bullet

Powder	Minimum Charge	Muzzle Velocity	Maximum Charge	Muzzle Velocity	Barrel Length
Lil'Gun	13.4 grains	2944 fps	14.9 grains	3155 fps	24" barrel
H322	19.7 grains	2883 fps	21.0 grains	3087 fps	24" barrel

Hodgdon Lil'Gun and H322 Powder—45-Grain Bullet

Powder	Minimum Charge	Muzzle Velocity	Maximum Charge	Muzzle Velocity	Barrel Length
Lil'Gun	13.8 grains	2964 fps	15.3 grains	3202 fps	24" barrel
H322	19.0 grains	2762 fps	20.5 grains	2978 fps	24" barrel

Hodgdon Lil'Gun and H322—50-Grain Bullet

Powder	Minimum Charge	Muzzle Velocity	Maximum Charge	Muzzle Velocity	Barrel Length
Lil'Gun	13.0 grains	2835 fps	14.6 grains	2994 fps	24" barrel
H322	19.0 grains	2703 fps	21.0 grains	2968 fps	24" barrel

Hodgdon Lil'Gun and H322—55-Grain Bullet

Powder	Minimum Charge	Muzzle Velocity	Maximum Charge	Muzzle Velocity	Barrel Length
Lil'Gun	13.0 grains	2714 fps	14.5 grains	2877 fps	24" barrel
H322	18.9 grains	2681 fps	21.0 grains	2944 fps	24" barrel

RANGE TESTS

When I performed range testing of the .221 Remington Fireball, it was a bright, sunny day and there was a moderate breeze from about 11 o'clock. The temperature was in the low 90s.

I used Remington's Premier AccuTip with the 50-grain AccuTip-V boat tail bullet for the factory ammo test. As can be seen from the test targets on the next page, this is accurate ammunition. For those of you who do not handload, I recommend you give this particular factory ammunition serious consideration. Group 1 measured 0.5" center to center and group 2 measured 0.68".

The printout from the Oehler Model 35P chronograph, also on the next page, shows that the average velocity of 2887 fps is about 100 fps lower than that claimed by Remington. And for some reason, only six of the ten shots fired were registered by my chronograph. This could have resulted from the bright sunlight. I think this is enough, though, to provide a reasonable measurement of the average velocity.

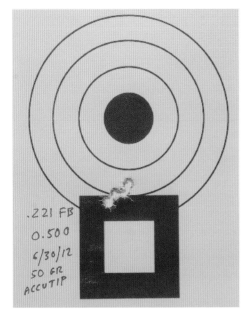

.221 Remington Fireball—Factory Ammo Group 1.

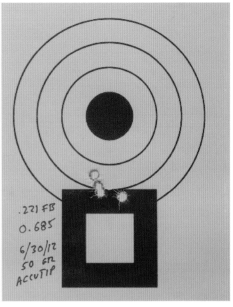

.221 Remington Fireball—Factory Ammo Group 2.

The printout from the Oehler 35P chronograph for the Remington factory ammunition indicates an average velocity (M) of 2887 fps and a standard deviation ($) of 24 fps.

The lower the standard deviation number, the better. And 24 fps indicates a consistent load.

```
2877-01-2875-
2863-02-2861-
2930-03-2926-
2871-04-2869-
2888-05-2886-
2960-06-2908-
-------
        06-2926-+
        06-2861--
        06-0065-T
        06-2887-M
        06-0024-$
-------
```

For my handload I chose the Sierra 40-grain BlitzKing bullet, 17.5 grains of IMR 4198 powder, and the Remington No. 7½ primer.

This load produced the following five-shot groups at 100 yards.

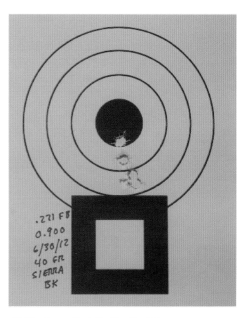

.221 Remington Fireball—Handload Group 1.

.221 Remington Fireball—Handload Group 2.

The first five-shot group for my handload measured 0.76" with four of the shots in 0.45". The second group measured 0.9" with four of the shots in 0.55". I believe that this handload has produced acceptable accuracy and warrants further testing.

For the handloads, the chronograph registered all ten shots. These results are on the next page.

According to the load tables, my load of 17.5 grains is approaching the maximum of 18.0 grains. I am pleased with the accuracy, so I think I'll stick with this load for now and contemplate working up loads with some of the new powders, such as Varget and Benchrest, in the future.

If you are not a handloader but would like to hunt varmints, the accuracy of factory ammunition for the .221 Remington Fireball is not a limitation. Unfortunately, though, you are limited to only a couple of choices: Nosler's Varmageddon or Remington's AccuTip.

As for factory varmint rifles chambered for the .221 Remington Fireball cartridge, the only one I'm currently aware of is CZ, which chambers this in its Model 527 American. Also, Cooper Arms includes the .221 Remington Fireball in its Model 21 series, including the Varminter. I consider my Cooper Model 21 Varminter in .221 Remington Fireball to be an excellent rifle for targeting varmints as small as a prairie dog at a maximum range of 300 yards. Why this accurate little cartridge is not offered in more factory rifles is a mystery to me. I suppose the wane in its popularity is due in part to the newer offering from Remington—the .17 Remington Fireball.

```
3581-01-3568-
3490-02-3478-
3502-03-3491-
3571-04-3558-
3565-05-3557-
3587-06-3568-
3623-07-3601-
3616-08-3598-
3590-09-3573-
3623-10-3603-
- -- -- -- -- -- -
    10-3603-+
    10-3478--
    10-0125-T
    10-3559-M
    10-0043-$
    -- -- -- -- -- -- -
```

The printout from the Oehler 35P chronograph for my handload indicates an average velocity (M) of 2952 fps and a standard deviation ($) of 24 fps. As with the reading for the factory ammo, 24 fps indicates a consistent load.

The average velocity reading of 2952 fps agrees quite closely with that published in the reloading manuals.

TRAJECTORY TABLES

The following trajectory tables were developed using the Handloads.com ballistic calculator. The tables are based on the line of sight (LOS) being 1.5 inches above the line of fire (LOF). All tabular data is expressed in inches.

40-Grain Bullet (BC = .196)

Muzzle Velocity (fps)	Muzzle	100 yards	200 yards	250 yards	300 yards
3300	−1.5	0.0	−3.0	−6.9	−12.6
	−1.5	1.5	0.0	−3.1	−8.0
	−1.5	2.8	2.4	0.0	−4.4
3200	−1.5	0.0	−3.4	−7.5	−13.7
	−1.5	1.7	0.0	−3.3	−8.7
	−1.5	3.0	2.6	0.0	−4.7
3100	−1.5	0.0	−3.7	−8.2	−14.9
	−1.5	1.9	0.0	−3.6	−9.4
	−1.5	3.3	2.8	0.0	−5.1
3000	−1.5	0.0	−4.1	−9.0	−16.3
	−1.5	2.0	0.0	−3.9	−10.1
	−1.5	3.6	3.1	0.0	−5.5
2900	−1.5	0.0	−4.5	−9.8	−17.7
	−1.5	2.2	0.0	−4.2	−11.0
	−1.5	3.9	3.3	0.0	−6.0
2800	−1.5	0.0	−5.0	−10.8	−19.4
	−1.5	2.5	0.0	−4.6	−12.0
	−1.5	4.3	3.6	0.0	−6.5

45-Grain Bullet (BC = .202)

Muzzle Velocity (fps)	Muzzle	100 yards	200 yards	250 yards	300 yards
	−1.5	0.0	−3.0	−6.8	−12.4
3300	−1.5	1.5	0.0	−3.0	−7.9
	−1.5	2.7	2.4	0.0	−4.3
	−1.5	0.0	−3.3	−7.4	−13.4
3200	−1.5	1.7	0.0	−3.2	−8.5
	−1.5	3.0	2.6	0.0	−4.6
	−1.5	0.0	−3.7	−8.0	−14.6
3100	−1.5	1.8	0.0	−3.5	−9.2
	−1.5	3.2	2.8	0.0	−5.0
	−1.5	0.0	−4.0	−8.8	−15.9
3000	−1.5	2.0	0.0	−3.8	−9.9
	−1.5	3.5	3.0	0.0	−5.4
	−1.5	0.0	−4.4	−9.6	−17.4
2900	−1.5	2.2	0.0	−4.1	−10.8
	−1.5	3.9	3.3	0.0	−5.8
	−1.5	0.0	−4.9	−10.6	−19.0
2800	−1.5	2.4	0.0	−4.5	−11.7
	−1.5	4.2	3.6	0.0	−6.4
	−1.5	0.0	−5.4	−11.6	−20.9
2700	−1.5	2.7	0.0	−4.9	−12.8
	−1.5	4.7	3.9	0.0	−6.9
	−1.5	0.0	−6.0	−12.8	−23.0
2600	−1.5	3.0	0.0	−5.3	−14.0
	−1.5	5.1	4.3	0.0	−7.6

50-Grain Bullet (BC = .243)

Muzzle Velocity (fps)	Muzzle	100 yards	200 yards	250 yards	300 yards
	−1.5	0.0	−3.7	−8.2	−14.9
3100	−1.5	1.9	0.0	−3.6	−9.4
	−1.5	3.3	2.8	0.0	−5.1
	−1.5	0.0	−4.1	−9.0	−16.3
3000	−1.5	2.0	0.0	−3.9	−10.1
	−1.5	3.6	3.1	0.0	−5.5
	−1.5	0.0	−4.5	−9.8	−17.7
2900	−1.5	2.2	0.0	−4.2	−11.0
	−1.5	3.9	3.3	0.0	−6.0
	−1.5	0.0	−5.0	−10.8	−19.4
2800	−1.5	2.5	0.0	−4.6	−12.0
	−1.5	4.3	3.6	0.0	−6.5
	−1.5	0.0	−5.5	−11.8	−21.3
2700	−1.5	2.8	0.0	−5.0	−13.1
	−1.5	4.7	4.0	0.0	−7.1
	−1.5	0.0	−6.1	−13.1	−23.4
2600	−1.5	3.0	0.0	−5.5	−14.3
	−1.5	5.2	4.4	0.0	−7.8

55-Grain Bullet (BC = .235)

Muzzle Velocity (fps)	Muzzle	100 yards	200 yards	250 yards	300 yards
	−1.5	0.0	−3.7	−8.1	−14.6
3000	−1.5	1.9	0.0	−3.5	−9.0
	−1.5	3.2	2.8	0.0	−4.8
	−1.5	0.0	−4.1	−8.9	−15.9
2900	−1.5	2.1	0.0	−3.7	−9.7
	−1.5	3.6	3.0	0.0	−5.2
	−1.5	0.0	−4.6	−9.8	−17.4
2800	−1.5	2.3	0.0	−4.1	−10.6
	−1.5	3.9	3.3	0.0	−5.7
	−1.5	0.0	−5.0	−10.7	−19.1
2700	−1.5	2.5	0.0	−4.4	−11.5
	−1.5	4.3	3.6	0.0	−6.2
	−1.5	0.0	−5.6	−11.8	−20.9
2600	−1.5	2.8	0.0	−4.9	−12.6
	−1.5	4.7	3.9	0.0	−6.8
	−1.5	0.0	−6.2	−13.1	−23.1
2500	−1.5	3.1	0.0	−5.3	−13.8
	−1.5	5.2	4.3	0.0	−7.4
	−1.5	0.0	−6.9	−14.5	−25.5
2400	−1.5	3.5	0.0	−5.9	−15.2
	−1.5	5.8	4.7	0.0	−8.2

Chapter 4
.223 Remington

The .223 Remington is, without a doubt, the most popular varmint cartridge of the current factory cartridges. It was developed by Remington in 1964 as the 5.56×45mm NATO round for use in the new M16 service rifle. In civilian garb, it's known as the .223 Remington. The cartridge is based on the .222 Remington, which was developed by Remington in 1950. The .223 case is only 0.06" longer than the .222 Remington, but it has greater powder capacity because the case body was lengthened by 0.174", which resulted in a shorter neck. The .223 Remington inherited the accuracy of the parent .222 Remington cartridge and is an excellent cartridge for shooting varmints at ranges up to 300 yards. And like the .222 Remington, the .223 Remington is a good choice for varmint shooting in areas that are somewhat settled.

THE COOPER MODEL 21 CUSTOM CLASSIC

The Model 21 Custom Classic from Cooper Firearms of Montana is truly a classic rifle. This rifle features an AAA Claro walnut stock with a hand-rubbed oil finish, genuine ebony fore-end tip, steel grip cap, Niedner butt plate, inletted swivel studs, and checkered bolt knob. All of the

metal is hand-polished to a high gloss and hot-blued. The 22 inch barrel has a sporter contour.

The checkering is a western fleur pattern. Besides being pleasing to the eye, this rifle, like all other Coopers, must shoot $\frac{1}{2}$" three-shot groups at 100 yards before leaving the factory.

Because this is a single-shot bolt action, there is no cutout in the bottom of the action or the stock for a magazine. The result is a stiffer action and stock, which enhances the accuracy of this rifle.

The trigger pull was adjusted to one pound. The trigger has no noticeable creep and breaks cleanly.

The scope is a Leupold VX-2 6-18×40mm with $\frac{1}{4}$ MOA windage and elevation adjustments. It has an adjustable objective for parallax correction and is mounted in Leupold medium height rings.

Like the CZ Model 527 American, the Cooper Custom Classic is also a good walking-around varmint rifle. The weight of the rifle, in combination with the scope and rings, is just less than eight pounds.

Rifling Twist Rates for the .223 Remington

The rifling twist for my Cooper Custom Classic in .223 Remington is 1:14". This twist rate should stabilize most bullet weights from 35 to 55 grains. The twist rate for the current .223

Author's Cooper Model 21 Custom Classic—.223 Remington.

Remington rifles from Cooper, as well as most other firearms manufacturers, has now been increased to 1:12" to stabilize bullets up to 65 grains. This faster twist rate may be too fast to stabilize some 35-grain bullets. You will need to experiment to determine if this is true.

Rifles chambered for the .223 Remington cartridge are available in more twist rates than those rifles for any other caliber because of the wide range of bullet weights (35 to 90 grains)

used. For varmint shooting, with bullets that range from 35 to 65 grains, a twist of 1:12" should suffice. However, rifles chambered for the 5.56mm NATO cartridge that are intended for use in service rifle competition at ranges up to 1,000 yards and use bullets that weigh up to 90 grains require a faster twist, depending on the bullet length and weight. The following table is a guide to determining which is the best twist rate based on your application.

.223 Remington/5.56mm NATO Rifling Twist Rates

Bullet Weights	Rifling Twist Rate	Application
35–55 grain	1:14	Varmint Shooting
40–65 grain	1:12	Varmint Shooting
69–75 grain	1:9 or 1:10	Hunting, Military, Tactical, and Target Competition
77–80 grain	1:7 or 1:8	Hunting, Military, Tactical, and Target Competition
90 grain	1:7	Target Competition

While the table is based on bullet weight, the bullet length is what actually influences the twist rate. It just so happens that, in most cases, the longer the bullet, the heavier its weight. A simple formula for determining the twist rate for a given bullet is:

Twist = 150 x D^2/L

Where:

D = bullet diameter in inches

L = bullet length in inches

150 = constant   (For muzzle velocities of more than 1800 fps, which invariably includes the .223 Remington, most ballistics experts suggest using a constant of 180)

For example, let's use the Sierra 52-grain match HPBT bullet, which has a length of 0.71".

The twist would be 180 ×(0.224 × 0.224) divided by 0.71, which equals 12.7. In this case, a twist of 1:12" or 1:14" would probably work equally well.

Another consideration is the case of loading a light bullet, such as the Hornady 40-grain V-MAX, in a rifle with a barrel twist faster than 1:12". Fired at a high muzzle velocity, say, 3700 fps, in a rifle having a twist of 1:7", it is possible that the bullet might disintegrate before reaching the target.

.223 REMINGTON FACTORY AMMO

Factory ammo for the .223 Remington is available from Barnes, Federal, Hornady, Nosler, Remington, and Winchester.

The .223 Remington cartridge is probably the most popular cartridge for varmint shooting today. It's the civilian version of the 5.56mm NATO military cartridge used in the M16 service rifle. This cartridge, when used with heavier 70- to 90-grain bullets, is also used to compete in service rifle matches at ranges up to 600 yards.

Barnes Vor-Tx Ammunition

Bullet Weight (Grains)	Bullet Type	Velocity (fps)					Energy (ft-lbs)				
		Muzzle	100 yards	200 yards	300 yards	400 yards	Muzzle	100 yards	200 yards	300 yards	400 yards
55	TSX	3240	2774	2353	1970	1629	1282	940	676	474	324

Federal Premium Ammunition

Bullet Weight (Grains)	Bullet Type	Velocity (fps)					Energy (ft-lbs)				
		Muzzle	100 yards	200 yards	300 yards	400 yards	Muzzle	100 yards	200 yards	300 yards	400 yards
40	Nosler Ballistic Tip	3700	3209	2770	2371	2007	1218	915	682	499	358
50	JHP	3325	2839	2402	2006	1653	1227	895	640	447	303
55	Sierra GameKing	3240	2847	2487	2154	1847	1282	990	755	566	417

Hornady Superformance Varmint Ammunition

Bullet Weight (Grains)	Bullet Type	Velocity (fps)					Energy (ft-lbs)				
		Muzzle	100 yards	200 yards	300 yards	400 yards	Muzzle	100 yards	200 yards	300 yards	400 yards
35	Hornady NTX	4000	3354	2795	2299	1858	1243	874	607	411	268
40	Hornady V-MAX	3800	3249	2762	2324	1928	1282	937	677	479	330
53	Hornady V-MAX	3465	3106	2775	2468	2180	1135	906	716	559	431
55	Hornady V-MAX	3240	2854	2500	2172	1871	1282	995	763	576	427

Nosler Trophy Grade Varmint Ammunition

Bullet Weight (Grains)	Bullet Type	Velocity (fps)					Energy (ft-lbs)				
		Muzzle	100 yards	200 yards	300 yards	400 yards	Muzzle	100 yards	200 yards	300 yards	400 yards
35	BTLF	3750	3214	2742	2315	1927	1093	803	584	416	289
40	BT	3700	3215	2784	2390	2030	1216	918	688	507	366
40	BTLF	3625	3146	2719	2330	1973	1167	879	657	482	346

Nosler Varmageddon Ammunition

Bullet Weight (Grains)	Bullet Type	Velocity (fps)					Energy (ft-lbs)				
		Muzzle	100 yards	200 yards	300 yards	400 yards	Muzzle	100 yards	200 yards	300 yards	400 yards
55	FBHP	3100	2647	2236	1864	1537	1173	856	611	424	289
55	FBSP	3100	2725	2380	2061	1768	1173	907	692	518	382

Remington Varmint Ammunition

Bullet Weight (Grains)	Bullet Type	Velocity (fps)					Energy (ft-lbs)				
		Muzzle	100 yards	200 yards	300 yards	400 yards	Muzzle	100 yards	200 yards	300 yards	400 yards
45	Disintegrator Varmint	3550	2911	2355	1865	1451	1259	847	554	347	210
50	AccuTip-V	3410	2989	2605	2252	1928	1291	992	753	563	413
55	Power-Lokt	3240	2773	2352	1969	1627	1282	939	675	473	323
55	Express Rifle	3240	2747	2304	1905	1554	1282	921	648	443	295

Winchester Varmint Ammunition

Bullet Weight (Grains)	Bullet Type	Velocity (fps)					Energy (ft-lbs)				
		Muzzle	100 yards	200 yards	300 yards	400 yards	Muzzle	100 yards	200 yards	300 yards	400 yards
35	Silvertip	3800	3251	2766	2330	1935	1110	813	588	417	287
45	USA-JHP	3600	3033	2533	2085	1687	1295	919	641	434	284
50	Silvertip	3410	2982	2593	2235	1907	1291	987	746	555	404
55	Silvertip	3240	2871	2531	2215	1923	1282	1006	782	599	451
55	Super-X	3240	2747	2304	1905	1554	1282	921	648	443	295

HANDLOADING THE .223 REMINGTON

All of the current reloading manuals list data for the .223 Remington. In addition to these manuals, Hodgdon publishes an annual reloading manual in magazine format that includes load data for the .223 Remington.

.223 Remington Versus 5.56 × 45mm NATO

Military rifles chambered for the 5.56×45mm NATO cartridge are built to NATO specs and have a longer throat that is optimized for shooting longer, heavier bullets. These rifles are rated at 60,000 CUP maximum pressure. Rifles chambered for the commercial .223

Remington cartridge are built to SAAMI specs, have a shorter throat, and are rated at 50,000 CUP maximum pressure. Also, military ammunition, while having the same outside dimensions as the commercial .223 Remington, may be constructed of thicker brass. This slightly reduces the case capacity as compared with commercial brass. In fact, some reloading manuals include data that distinguishes between the .223 Remington and 5.56×45mm NATO cartridges. If you will be reloading this cartridge using military brass, please be aware of these differences.

Barnes Reloading Manual Number 4

The Barnes manual lists loads for the company's 36-, 45-, 53-, 62-, and 70-grain bullets. For each bullet weight, Barnes identifies the powder that produces the most accurate loads. For example, Accurate's XMR 2015 produced the most accurate loads for the 45-grain bullet, and Hodgdon's H4895 powder was the most accurate load for the Barnes 53-grain TSX FB bullet.

Barnes notes that a twist of 1:12" or faster is required to stabilize the 45-grain Banded Solid Spitzer and 53-grain TSX bullets. A twist rate of 1:9" or faster is needed for the Barnes 62-grain TSX bullet; a twist of 1:8" or faster is required for the 70-grain TSX bullet.

Hornady Handbook of Cartridge Reloading, 8th Edition

The Hornady manual lists separate service rifle data for the .223 Remington. This data includes load tables for the 68- and 75-grain Hornady bullets and is based on loads tested in a Colt AR-15 rifle with a 20 inch Citadel barrel having a 1:9" twist.

The data for the commercial version of the .223 Remington is from tests using a Remington Model 700 rifle having a 26 inch barrel with a 1:12" twist. Since we are handloading for varmint shooting, we will refer to the load tables for the commercial version. IMR 4198, TAC, H335, Benchmark, and BL-C(2) powders are listed for all of the Hornady bullets in these load tables. IMR 4895 and H322 are listed for the 50-, 52-, 53-, and 55-grain bullets. The most uniform velocity and best accuracy for all bullet weights was achieved using IMR 4198, Vihtavuori N130 and N135, and H322 powders.

Lyman Reloading Handbook, 49th Edition

The Lyman manual lists .223 Remington loads for bullet weights from 36 to 80 grains. For our purpose, we will consider the load data for the 50-, 52-, and 55-grain bullets. Lyman's best accuracy for the 50-grain Sierra Blitz bullet was obtained with AA2015 powder. Benchmark proved the most accurate powder for the Sierra 52-grain HPBT bullet, and Varget was the most accurate powder for the Sierra 55-grain SPT bullet. Lyman's test data was based on its Universal Receiver using a 24 inch barrel with a 1:12" twist.

Norma Reloading Manual Edition No. 1

While the Norma manual includes data for bullet weights of 50, 52, 55, 60, and 69 grains, as a powder manufacturing company it lists only Norma powders in the load tables. For the 50-, 52-, and 55-grain bullets, load data is given for the Norma 200 and 201 powders. For the 60-grain bullet, load data is listed for Norma's 200, 201, and 202 powders. Data for the 69-grain bullet includes Norma 201, 202, and 203-B powders.

Nosler Reloading Guide No. 6

Like the Hornady manual, the Nosler manual also provides separate data for the commercial .223 Remington and the 5.56×45mm NATO cartridges. For our purpose, which is developing varmint loads, we will refer only to the .233 Remington data. For its testing, Nosler used a 24 inch barrel with a twist rate of 1:12".

The most accurate powder for the Nosler 40-grain Solid Base Ballistic Tip bullet was Winchester's W748. The most accurate charge for this powder was the maximum of 27 grains. For the Nosler 50- and 52-grain bullets, Benchmark powder proved the most accurate. For the 55-grain Solid Base Ballistic Tip and CT Ballistic Silvertip bullets, the most accurate powder tested was Hodgdon's H335. And for the Nosler 60-grain Partition Spitzer bullet, 22.5 grains of Benchmark powder gave the best accuracy.

Sierra 5th Edition Reloading Manual

The Sierra manual also publishes two separate sets of data for the .223 Remington—one for use in bolt-action rifles and the other for use in semiautomatic rifles, such as the AR-15. For the purpose of this book, however, I will only refer to the data listed for bolt-action rifles.

For those of you who choose to shoot varmints with a semiautomatic, which can be as accurate as a bolt action, you are certainly welcome to refer to the AR-15 data in the Sierra manual. The data in this section of the manual was based on testing with a Colt AR-15A2 HBAR with a rifling twist of 1:7".

Referring to the data in the bolt-action section, Sierra includes load tables for its 40-, 45-, 50-, 52/53-, 55-, 60-, 63-, 69-, and 80-grain bullets, the latter two being for match competition. Sierra's accuracy load for 40-grain bullets was with 23 grains of IMR 4198 and, for hunting, 29.1 grains of H335. The best accuracy for the Sierra 45-grain Hornet and SPT bullets was with 27.6 grains of H335 powder, or for hunting, 27.1 grains of Vihtavuori N135. Hodgdon's H335 also produced the best results for both accuracy, at 27.3 grains, and hunting, at 28.0 grains, with the Sierra 50-grain bullets. This powder proved the most accurate for the 52- and 53-grain MatchKing bullets at 26.9 grains, as well. The best accuracy for the 55-grain bullets was achieved with 24.2 grains of Vihtavuori N133 powder, and the recommended hunting

load was with 26.1 grains of H4895. The Sierra 60-grain HP bullet gave the best accuracy with 23.2 grains of AA2015 powder; the recommended hunting load was 26.7 grains of Hodgdon's Varget powder. The Sierra 63-grain SMP bullet produced the best accuracy with 20.5 grains of RE-7, and Sierra recommended 23.3 grains of Vihtavuori N133 powder for a hunting load with this bullet.

The data for the bolt-action section of the Sierra manual was based on testing using a Remington 600 rifle with a 24 inch barrel having a rifling twist of 1:14".

Speer Reloading Manual #14

The Speer manual includes .223 Remington loads for its 40-, 45-, 50-, 52-, 55-, 62-, and 70-grain bullets. Speer includes powders that most of the other manuals list, but does not identify any powders as producing the best accuracy. Its test firearm was a Remington Model 40-X with a 24 inch barrel. It does not list the rifling twist in the test rifle's barrel.

The following tables list some loads from the current reloading manuals for each bullet weight from 40 to 55 grains. I consider these weights suitable for varmint shooting with the .223 Remington. I have not included data from the Norma manual because it lists loads only for the Norma powders. If you have a supply of these powders, I recommend you consult the *Norma Reloading Manual*, 1st edition, for load data.

For the .223 Remington, I am going to try the following load: Sierra 52-grain HPBT Match bullet, 25 grains of IMR 4895 powder, Remington No. 7½ primer, and Winchester brass.

Hodgdon Benchmark Powder—40-Grain Bullet*

Manual	Minimum Charge	Muzzle Velocity	Maximum Charge	Muzzle Velocity	Barrel Length, Twist Rate
Hornady	24.7 grains	3300 fps	26.4 grains	3500 fps	26" barrel, 1:12"
Lyman	25.2 grains	3276 fps	28.0 grains	3627 fps	24" barrel, 1:12"
Nosler	26.0 grains	3602 fps	28.0 grains	3860 fps	24" barrel, 1:12"

*The Barnes manual does not list loads for the 40-grain bullet. The Sierra and Speer manuals do not list Benchmark powder.

Hodgdon Benchmark Powder—45-Grain Bullet*

Manual	Minimum Charge	Muzzle Velocity	Maximum Charge	Muzzle Velocity	Barrel Length, Twist Rate
Barnes	24.0 grains	3185 fps	26.0 grains	3521 fps	24" barrel, 1:12"
Hornady	23.7 grains	3100 fps	26.4 grains	3500 fps	26" barrel, 1:12"
Lyman	24.7 grains	3173 fps	27.5 grains	3480 fps	24" barrel, 1:12"

*The Nosler manual does not list loads for 45-grain bullets. The Sierra and Speer manuals do not list Benchmark powder.

Hodgdon Benchmark Powder—50-Grain Bullet*

Manual	Minimum Charge	Muzzle Velocity	Maximum Charge	Muzzle Velocity	Barrel Length, Twist Rate
Hornady	21.5 grains	2900 fps	25.8 grains	3300 fps	26" barrel, 1:12"
Lyman	23.8 grains	3043 fps	26.5 grains	3332 fps	24" barrel, 1:12"
Nosler	24.5 grains	3285 fps	26.5 grains	3540 fps	24" barrel, 1:12"

*The Barnes manual does not list Benchmark powder for its 50-grain bullet. The Sierra and Speer manuals do not list Benchmark powder.

Hodgdon Benchmark Powder—52/53-Grain Bullets*

Manual	Minimum Charge	Muzzle Velocity	Maximum Charge	Muzzle Velocity	Barrel Length, Twist Rate
Hornady	22.1 grains	2900 fps	25.0 grains	3200 fps	26" barrel, 1:12"
Lyman	23.1 grains	2932 fps	25.7 grains	3251 fps	24" barrel, 1:12"
Nosler	24.5 grains	3285 fps	26.5 grains	3540 fps	24" barrel, 1:12"

*The Barnes manual does not list Benchmark powder for its 53-grain bullet. The Sierra and Speer manuals do not list Benchmark powder.

Hodgdon Benchmark Powder—55-Grain Bullet*

Manual	Minimum Charge	Muzzle Velocity	Maximum Charge	Muzzle Velocity	Barrel Length, Twist Rate
Hornady	21.6 grains	2800 fps	24.5 grains	3100 fps	26" barrel, 1:12"
Lyman	22.7 grains	2793 fps	25.3 grains	3137 fps	24" barrel, 1:12"
Nosler	23.0 grains	3050 fps	25.0 grains	3302 fps	24" barrel, 1:12"

*The Barnes manual does not list a 55-grain bullet. The Sierra and Speer manuals do not list Benchmark powder.

IMR 4198 Powder—40-Grain Bullet*

Manual	Minimum Charge	Muzzle Velocity	Maximum Charge	Muzzle Velocity	Barrel Length, Twist Rate
Hornady	19.3 grains	3300 fps	22.2 grains	3700 fps	26" barrel, 1:12"
Lyman	20.6 grains	3170 fps	22.9 grains	3545 fps	24" barrel, 1:12"
Nosler	21.0 grains	3302 fps	23.0 grains	3682 fps	24" barrel, 1:12"
Sierra	21.5 grains	3200 fps	23.5 grains	3600 fps	24" barrel, 1:14"
Speer	20.5 grains	2981 fps	22.5 grains	3342 fps	22" barrel

*The Barnes manual does not list loads for the 40-grain bullet. The Speer manual lists H4198 powder, which is similar to IMR 4198 powder but not identical in burning characteristics.

IMR 4198 Powder—45-Grain Bullet*

Manual	Minimum Charge	Muzzle Velocity	Maximum Charge	Muzzle Velocity	Barrel Length, Twist Rate
Barnes	20.0 grains	3126 fps	22.0 grains	3479 fps	24" barrel, 1:12"
Hornady	20.6 grains	3100 fps	22.7 grains	3400 fps	26" barrel, 1:12"
Lyman	20.6 grains	3171 fps	22.9 grains	3542 fps	24" barrel, 1:12"
Sierra	21.2 grains	3200 fps	23.2 grains	3600 fps	24" barrel, 1:14"
Speer	21.0 grains	3006 fps	23.0 grains	3377 fps	22" barrel

*The Nosler manual does not list a 45-grain bullet.

IMR 4198 Powder—50-Grain Bullet*

Manual	Minimum Charge	Muzzle Velocity	Maximum Charge	Muzzle Velocity	Barrel Length, Twist Rate
Hornady	19.5 grains	2900 fps	22.2 grains	3300 fps	26" barrel, 1:12"
Lyman	20.0 grains	2739 fps	22.0 grains	3115 fps	24" barrel, 1:12"
Nosler	20.0 grains	2990 fps	22.0 grains	3230 fps	24" barrel, 1:12"
Sierra	20.1 grains	3000 fps	22.9 grains	3400 fps	24" barrel, 1:14"

*The Barnes manual does not list loads for the 50-grain bullet. The Speer manual does not list IMR 4198 powder for the 50-grain bullet.

IMR 4198 Powder—52/53-Grain Bullets*

Manual	Minimum Charge	Muzzle Velocity	Maximum Charge	Muzzle Velocity	Barrel Length, Twist Rate
Hornady	19.2 grains	2900 fps	21.9 grains	3200 fps	26" barrel, 1:12"
Lyman	19.0 grains	2666 fps	21.6 grains	3039 fps	24" barrel, 1:12"
Nosler	20.0 grains	2990 fps	22.0 grains	3230 fps	24" barrel, 1:12"
Sierra	19.6 grains	2900 fps	22.4 grains	3300 fps	24" barrel, 1:14"

*The Barnes manual does not list IMR 4198 powder for its 53-grain bullet. The Speer manual does not list IMR 4198 powder for the 52/53-grain bullets.

IMR 4198 Powder—55-Grain Bullet*

Manual	Minimum Charge	Muzzle Velocity	Maximum Charge	Muzzle Velocity	Barrel Length, Twist Rate
Hornady	17.4 grains	2800 fps	20.0 grains	3100 fps	26" barrel, 1:12"
Lyman	19.0 grains	2645 fps	21.7 grains	3067 fps	24" barrel, 1:12"
Nosler	19.5 grains	2930 fps	21.5 grains	3170 fps	24" barrel, 1:12"
Sierra	19.2 grains	2800 fps	22.0 grains	3200 fps	24" barrel, 1:14"

*The Barnes manual does not list a 55-grain bullet. The Speer manual does not list IMR 4198 powder for the 55-grain bullet.

Hodgdon H322 Powder—40-Grain Bullet*

Manual	Minimum Charge	Muzzle Velocity	Maximum Charge	Muzzle Velocity	Barrel Length, Twist Rate
Lyman	24.3 grains	3095 fps	27.0 grains	3619 fps	24" barrel, 1:12"
Nosler	23.0 grains	3302 fps	25.0 grains	3567 fps	24" barrel, 1:12"
Sierra	24.1 grains	3200 fps	25.5 grains	3400 fps	24" barrel, 1:14"
Speer	24.0 grains	3027 fps	26.0 grains	3388 fps	22" barrel

*The Barnes manual does not list loads for the 40-grain bullet. The Hornady manual does not list H322 powder for the 40-grain bullet.

Hodgdon H322 Powder—45-Grain Bullet*

Manual	Minimum Charge	Muzzle Velocity	Maximum Charge	Muzzle Velocity	Barrel Length, Twist Rate
Hornady	23.3 grains	3100 fps	25.1 grains	3400 fps	26" barrel, 1:12"
Lyman	24.4 grains	3274 fps	27.2 grains	3571 fps	24" barrel, 1:12"
Sierra	22.6 grains	3100 fps	25.3 grains	3400 fps	24" barrel, 1:14"
Speer	24.0 grains	2959 fps	26.0 grains	3362 fps	22" barrel

*The Barnes manual does not list H322 powder for its 55-grain bullet. The Nosler manual does not list a 45-grain bullet.

Hodgdon H322 Powder—50-Grain Bullet*

Manual	Minimum Charge	Muzzle Velocity	Maximum Charge	Muzzle Velocity	Barrel Length, Twist Rate
Hornady	21.9 grains	2900 fps	25.2 grains	3400 fps	26" barrel, 1:12"
Sierra	22.8 grains	3000 fps	24.9 grains	3300 fps	24" barrel, 1:14"
Speer	24.0 grains	3001 fps	26.0 grains	3300 fps	22" barrel

*The Barnes, Lyman, and Nosler manuals do not list H322 powder for their 50-grain bullets.

Hodgdon H322 Powder—52/53-Grain Bullets*

Manual	Minimum Charge	Muzzle Velocity	Maximum Charge	Muzzle Velocity	Barrel Length, Twist Rate
Hornady	22.2 grains	2900 fps	25.0 grains	3300 fps	26" barrel, 1:12"
Sierra	22.5 grains	3000 fps	24.3 grains	3200 fps	24" barrel, 1:14"
Speer	22.5 grains	2822 fps	24.5 grains	3101 fps	22" barrel

*The Barnes, Lyman, and Nosler manuals do not list H322 powder for their 52/53-grain bullets.

Hodgdon H322 Powder—55-Grain Bullet*

Manual	Minimum Charge	Muzzle Velocity	Maximum Charge	Muzzle Velocity	Barrel Length, Twist Rate
Hornady	19.5 grains	2800 fps	23.1 grains	3100 fps	26" barrel, 1:12"
Sierra	22.1 grains	2800 fps	23.9 grains	3100 fps	24" barrel, 1:14"
Speer	22.5 grains	2823 fps	24.5 grains	3158 fps	22" barrel

*The Barnes manual does not list a 55-grain bullet. The Lyman and Nosler manuals do not list H322 powder for their 55-grain bullets.

Hodgdon VARGET Powder—40-Grain Bullet*

Manual	Minimum Charge	Muzzle Velocity	Maximum Charge	Muzzle Velocity	Barrel Length, Twist Rate
Lyman	25.6 grains	3042 fps	28.0 grains	3383 fps	24" barrel, 1:12"
Nosler	25.0 grains	3111 fps	27.0 grains	3383 fps	24" barrel, 1:12"
Sierra	26.2 grains	3200 fps	27.2 grains	3400 fps	24" barrel, 1:14"
Speer	26.0 grains	3148 fps	28.0 grains	3461 fps	22" barrel

*The Barnes manual does not list loads for the 40-grain bullet. The Hornady manual does not list Varget powder for the 40-grain bullet.

Hodgdon VARGET Powder—45-Grain Bullet*

Manual	Minimum Charge	Muzzle Velocity	Maximum Charge	Muzzle Velocity	Barrel Length, Twist Rate
Lyman	25.2 grains	3023 fps	28.0 grains	3369 fps	24" barrel, 1:12"
Sierra	25.7 grains	3100 fps	26.9 grains	3300 fps	24" barrel, 1:14"
Speer	26.0 grains	3109 fps	28.0 grains	3387 fps	22" barrel

*The Barnes and Hornady manuals do not list Varget powder for the 45-grain bullets. The Nosler manual does not list a 45-grain bullet.

Hodgdon VARGET Powder—50-Grain Bullet*

Manual	Minimum Charge	Muzzle Velocity	Maximum Charge	Muzzle Velocity	Barrel Length, Twist Rate
Lyman	25.4 grains	3010 fps	28.2 grains	3376 fps	24" barrel, 1:12"
Sierra	25.2 grains	3000 fps	26.8 grains	3200 fps	24" barrel, 1:14"
Speer	25.5 grains	3034 fps	27.5 grains	3316 fps	22" barrel

*The Barnes, Hornady, and Nosler manuals do not list Varget powder for the 50-grain bullets.

Hodgdon VARGET Powder—52/53-Grain Bullets*

Manual	Minimum Charge	Muzzle Velocity	Maximum Charge	Muzzle Velocity	Barrel Length, Twist Rate
Barnes	24.5 grains	3026 fps	26.5 grains	3247 fps	24" barrel, 1:12"
Hornady	23.3 grains	2900 fps	26.0 grains	3200 fps	26" barrel, 1:12"
Lyman	25.6 grains	3019 fps	28.0 grains	3377 fps	24" barrel, 1:12"
Sierra	24.3 grains	2900 fps	26.7 grains	3200 fps	24" barrel, 1:14"
Speer	25.0 grains	2995 fps	27.0 grains	3276 fps	22" barrel

*The Nosler manual does not list Varget powder for the 52/53-grain bullets.

Hodgdon VARGET Powder—55-Grain Bullet*

Manual	Minimum Charge	Muzzle Velocity	Maximum Charge	Muzzle Velocity	Barrel Length, Twist Rate
Hornady	22.8 grains	2800 fps	26.4 grains	3200 fps	26" barrel, 1:12"
Lyman	25.0 grains	2977 fps	27.8 grains	3346 fps	24" barrel, 1:12"
Nosler	23.0 grains	2805 fps	25.0 grains	3037 fps	24" barrel, 1:12"
Sierra	23.7 grains	2800 fps	26.9 grains	3200 fps	24" barrel, 1:14"
Speer	25.0 grains	2969 fps	27.0 grains	3216 fps	22" barrel

*The Barnes manual does not list a 55-grain bullet.

Hodgdon H335 Powder—40-Grain Bullet*

Manual	Minimum Charge	Muzzle Velocity	Maximum Charge	Muzzle Velocity	Barrel Length, Twist Rate
Hornady	24.3 grains	3300 fps	27.4 grains	3700 fps	26" barrel, 1:12"
Lyman	25.5 grains	3135 fps	28.3 grains	3640 fps	24" barrel, 1:12"
Nosler	25.5 grains	3406 fps	27.5 grains	3681 fps	24" barrel, 1:12"
Sierra	25.6 grains	3200 fps	29.1 grains	3700 fps	24" barrel, 1:14"
Speer	26.5 grains	2903 fps	28.5 grains	3133 fps	22" barrel

*The Barnes manual does not list loads for the 40-grain bullet.

Hodgdon H335 Powder—45-Grain Bullet*

Manual	Minimum Charge	Muzzle Velocity	Maximum Charge	Muzzle Velocity	Barrel Length, Twist Rate
Hornady	23.0 grains	3100 fps	27.1 grains	3500 fps	26" barrel, 1:12"
Lyman	26.1 grains	3200 fps	29.4 grains	3678 fps	24" barrel, 1:12"
Sierra	24.8 grains	3100 fps	28.3 grains	3600 fps	24" barrel, 1:14"
Speer	25.0 grains	2688 fps	27.0 grains	3020 fps	22" barrel

*The Barnes manual does not list H335 powder. The Nosler manual does not list a 45-grain bullet.

Hodgdon H335 Powder—50-Grain Bullet*

Manual	Minimum Charge	Muzzle Velocity	Maximum Charge	Muzzle Velocity	Barrel Length, Twist Rate
Hornady	21.8 grains	2900 fps	25.7 grains	3300 fps	26" barrel, 1:12"
Lyman	24.8 grains	3025 fps	27.7 grains	3459 fps	24" barrel, 1:12"
Nosler	24.0 grains	3080 fps	26.0 grains	3260 fps	24" barrel, 1:12"
Sierra	24.5 grains	3000 fps	28.0 grains	3500 fps	24" barrel, 1:14"
Speer	25.0 grains	2975 fps	27.0 grains	3262 fps	22" barrel

*The Barnes manual does not list H335 powder.

Hodgdon H335 Powder—52/53-Grain Bullets*

Manual	Minimum Charge	Muzzle Velocity	Maximum Charge	Muzzle Velocity	Barrel Length, Twist Rate
Hornady	22.3 grains	2900 fps	25.4 grains	3200 fps	26" barrel, 1:12"
Lyman	24.5 grains	2950 fps	27.2 grains	3361 fps	24" barrel, 1:12"
Nosler	24.0 grains	3080 fps	26.0 grains	3260 fps	24" barrel, 1:12"
Sierra	24.1 grains	2900 fps	27.6 grains	3400 fps	24" barrel, 1:14"
Speer	24.5 grains	2879 fps	26.5 grains	3129 fps	22" barrel

*The Barnes manual does not list H335 powder.

Hodgdon H335 Powder—55-Grain Bullet*

Manual	Minimum Charge	Muzzle Velocity	Maximum Charge	Muzzle Velocity	Barrel Length, Twist Rate
Hornady	20.8 grains	2800 fps	23.2 grains	3100 fps	26" barrel, 1:12"
Lyman	24.3 grains	3142 fps	27.0 grains	3270 fps	24" barrel, 1:12"
Nosler	23.0 grains	2920 fps	25.0 grains	3140 fps	24" barrel, 1:12"
Sierra	23.0 grains	2800 fps	27.5 grains	3300 fps	24" barrel, 1:14"
Speer	24.0 grains	2805 fps	26.0 grains	3092 fps	22" barrel

*The Barnes manual does not list H335 powder.

IMR 4895 Powder—40-Grain Bullet*

Manual	Minimum Charge	Muzzle Velocity	Maximum Charge	Muzzle Velocity	Barrel Length, Twist Rate
Lyman	25.0 grains	3001 fps	27.8 grains	3444 fps	24" barrel, 1:12"
Speer	23.5 grains	2954 fps	25.5 grains	3297 fps	22" barrel

*The Barnes manual does not list loads for the 40-grain bullet. The Hornady, Nosler, and Sierra manuals do not list IMR 4895 powder for the 40-grain bullet. The Speer manual lists H4895 powder, which is similar to IMR 4895 powder but not identical in burning characteristics.

53

IMR 4895 Powder—45-Grain Bullet*

Manual	Minimum Charge	Muzzle Velocity	Maximum Charge	Muzzle Velocity	Barrel Length, Twist Rate
Lyman	25.2 grains	3009 fps	28.1 grains	3420 fps	24" barrel, 1:12"
Sierra	24.8 grains	3100 fps	27.2 grains	3500 fps	24" barrel, 1:14"
Speer	25.0 grains	3098 fps	27.0 grains	3404 fps	22" barrel

*The Barnes and Hornady manuals do not list IMR 4895 powder for the 45-grain bullet. The Sierra manual lists H4895 powder, which is similar to IMR 4895 powder but not identical in burning characteristics. The Nosler manual does not list a 45-grain bullet.

IMR 4895 Powder—50-Grain Bullet*

Manual	Minimum Charge	Muzzle Velocity	Maximum Charge	Muzzle Velocity	Barrel Length, Twist Rate
Hornady	24.3 grains	2900 fps	27.0 grains	3300 fps	26" barrel, 1:12"
Lyman	23.0 grains	2570 fps	26.5 grains	3115 fps	24" barrel, 1:12"
Nosler	24.0 grains	3040 fps	26.0 grains	3256 fps	24" barrel, 1:12"
Sierra	24.4 grains	3000 fps	26.8 grains	3400 fps	24" barrel, 1:14"
Speer	25.0 grains	3028 fps	27.0 grains	3313 fps	22" barrel

*The Barnes manual does not list IMR powder for the 50-grain bullet. The Sierra manual lists H4895 powder, which is similar to IMR 4895 powder but not identical in burning characteristics.

IMR 4895 Powder—52/53-Grain Bullets*

Manual	Minimum Charge	Muzzle Velocity	Maximum Charge	Muzzle Velocity	Barrel Length, Twist Rate
Barnes	23.5 grains	2970 fps	25.5 grains	3292 fps	24" barrel, 1:12"
Hornady	24.1 grains	2900 fps	27.1 grains	3300 fps	26" barrel, 1:12"
Lyman	23.0 grains	2538 fps	26.5 grains	3086 fps	24" barrel, 1:12"
Nosler	24.0 grains	3040 fps	26.0 grains	3256 fps	24" barrel, 1:12"
Sierra	23.8 grains	2900 fps	26.8 grains	3400 fps	24" barrel, 1:14"
Speer	24.5 grains	2850 fps	26.5 grains	3202 fps	22" barrel

*The Barnes and Sierra manuals list H4895 powder, which is similar to IMR 4895 powder but not identical in burning characteristics.

IMR 4895 Powder—55-Grain Bullet*

Manual	Minimum Charge	Muzzle Velocity	Maximum Charge	Muzzle Velocity	Barrel Length, Twist Rate
Hornady	22.7 grains	2800 fps	25.1 grains	3100 fps	26" barrel, 1:12"
Lyman	23.0 grains	2564 fps	26.0 grains	3030 fps	24" barrel, 1:12"
Nosler	23.5 grains	2988 fps	25.5 grains	3178 fps	24" barrel, 1:12"
Sierra	23.1 grains	2800 fps	26.1 grains	3300 fps	24" barrel, 1:14"
Speer	23.5 grains	2908 fps	25.5 grains	3194 fps	22" barrel

*The Barnes manual does not list loads for the 55-grain bullet. The Sierra and Speer manuals list H4895 powder, which is similar to IMR 4895 powder but not identical in burning characteristics.

RANGE TESTS

The range tests for the .223 Remington were performed on the same day as those with the .204 Ruger. There was a variable breeze from 12 o'clock, the temperature was in the high 80s, and the sun was bright.

The ammunition I selected for the factory test was the Federal Premium Vital-Shok with a 55-grain Triple-Shock bullet. This is premium ammo and sells for a premium price. I became concerned, however, after firing the first three rounds at the target. The Cooper is an accurate rifle; I have shot some groups with handloads in the past that measured under $\frac{1}{2}$ MOA. When I checked the first five-shot group through my spotting scope, I was shocked. It resembled one of my 25-yard handgun groups! It measured 3.62" center to center. I decided to continue the testing and fired another five-shot group. This one was even worse! It measured 6.25", with four shots in 3.28"—not at all what I would expect from premium ammunition.

I checked my scope mounting, and everything seemed tight. Could something have happened to my scope internally?

The chronograph data showed an average velocity for the ten shots of 3173 fps, which seemed okay, but the standard deviation was on the high side—102 fps.

At this time, I decided to test my handload to make sure something hadn't gone seriously wrong with the scope or rifle. My handload consisted of the Sierra 52-grain hollow point boat tail bullet, 25 grains of IMR 4895 powder, and the Remington No. $7\frac{1}{2}$ primer. The first five-shot group measured 0.54" and the second measured 0.88", with four shots in 0.58". It was a relief to see small groups return and know my rifle and scope were okay.

Like my CZ Model 527, the Cooper Model 21 Classic is a good choice for a walking-around varmint rifle. And the .223 Remington is, without a doubt, an excellent cartridge for all varmints out to 300 yards.

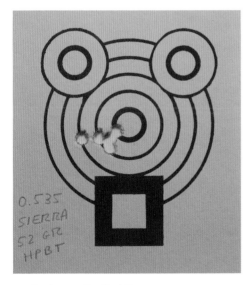

.223 Remington—Handload Group 1.

.223 Remington—Handload Group 2.

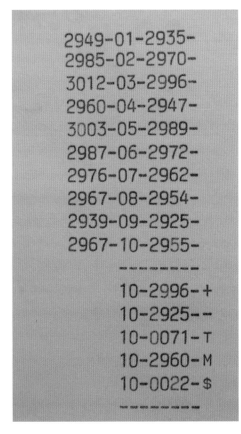

```
2949-01-2935-
2985-02-2970-
3012-03-2996-
2960-04-2947-
3003-05-2989-
2987-06-2972-
2976-07-2962-
2967-08-2954-
2939-09-2925-
2967-10-2955-
------------
10-2996-+
10-2925--
10-0071-T
10-2960-M
10-0022-$
------------
```

The Oehler 35P chronograph data for the .223 Remington handloads indicates an average velocity (M) of 2960 fps and a standard deviation (S) of 22 fps.

This velocity compares favorably with the data provided in the various reloading manuals.

I decided to try another brand for a second test of .223 Remington factory ammo. I selected Hornady's Superformance Varmint ammunition. This particular load used the Hornady 53-grain V-MAX bullet. To my chagrin, this ammo didn't perform much better than the Federal Premium in my Cooper. The two groups, five shots each, with the Hornady ammo measured 3.6" and 3.5", respectively. The chronograph showed an average muzzle velocity of 3328 fps and a standard deviation of 21, which indicates good load consistency. Again, I don't understand the large group sizes.

I had one other brand of factory ammo in my .223 Remington inventory—Remington's Express Rifle ammo, which used the Remington 55-grain pointed soft point bullet. This would not be regarded as premium ammunition, but I decided to try still a third test of factory ammo. The first group measured 1.84" with four shots in 1.6"; group 2 measured 1.95" with four shots in 1.2".

.223 Remington—Factory Group 1.

.223 Remington—Factory Group 2.

This still isn't good accuracy, but it is a slight improvement over the first two factory brands.

For some reason, which I am at a loss to explain, my rifle just doesn't like factory ammo. This makes a good argument for handloading.

```
3003-01-3005-
3003-02-3006-
3025-03-3026-
3044-04-3047-
3041-05-3044-
3037-06-3039-
3018-07-3016-
3072-08-3071-
3084-09-3086-
3048-10-3048-
---------
10-3086-+
10-3005--
10-0081-T
10-3038-M
10-0026-$
---------
```

The Oehler 35P chronograph data for the .223 Remington factory ammo measures an average velocity (M) of 3038 fps and a standard deviation ($) of 26 fps. This low a deviation indicates a uniform load.

The muzzle velocity, however, is about 200 fps lower than Remington's data.

TRAJECTORY TABLES

The following trajectory tables were developed using the Handloads.com ballistic calculator. The tables are based on the line of sight (LOS) being 1.5 inches above the line of fire (LOF). All tabular data is expressed in inches.

40-Grain Bullet (BC = .155)

Muzzle Velocity (fps)	Muzzle	100 yards	200 yards	300 yards	400 yards
	−1.5	0.0	−2.2	−10.3	−27.7
3800	−1.5	1.1	0.0	−6.9	−23.3
	−1.5	3.4	4.6	0.0	−14.0
	−1.5	0.0	−2.5	−11.1	−29.8
3700	−1.5	1.2	0.0	−7.4	−24.8
	−1.5	3.4	4.9	0.0	−15.0
	−1.5	0.0	−2.7	−12.0	−32.0
3600	−1.5	1.4	0.0	−7.9	−26.6
	−1.5	4.0	5.3	0.0	−16.0
	−1.5	0.0	−3.0	−12.9	−34.4
3500	−1.5	1.5	0.0	−8.5	−28.5
	−1.5	4.3	5.7	0.0	−17.2
	−1.5	0.0	−3.2	−14.0	−37.1
3400	−1.5	1.6	0.0	−9.1	−30.7
	−1.5	4.7	6.1	0.0	−18.5
	−1.5	0.0	−3.5	−15.1	−40.1
3300	−1.5	1.8	0.0	−9.8	−33.0
	−1.5	5.1	6.6	0.0	−19.9

45-Grain Bullet (BC = .210)

Muzzle Velocity (fps)	Muzzle	100 yards	200 yards	300 yards	400 yards
	−1.5	0.0	−2.4	−10.3	−25.8
3500	−1.5	1.2	0.0	−6.7	−20.9
	−1.5	3.4	4.4	0.0	−12.1
	−1.5	0.0	−2.7	−11.1	−27.8
3400	−1.5	1.3	0.0	−7.1	−22.5
	−1.5	3.7	4.8	0.0	−13.0
	−1.5	0.0	−2.9	−12.1	−30.0
3300	−1.5	1.5	0.0	−7.7	−24.1
	−1.5	4.0	5.1	0.0	−13.9
	−1.5	0.0	−3.2	−13.1	−32.5
3200	−1.5	1.6	0.0	−8.3	−26.0
	−1.5	4.4	5.5	0.0	−15.0
	−1.5	0.0	−3.6	−14.3	−35.2
3100	−1.5	1.8	0.0	−8.9	−28.1
	−1.5	4.8	5.9	0.0	−16.2

50-Grain Bullet (BC = .222)

Muzzle Velocity (fps)	Muzzle	100 yards	200 yards	300 yards	400 yards
3400	−1.5	0.0	−2.5	−10.3	−25.1
	−1.5	1.2	0.0	−6.5	−20.1
	−1.5	3.4	4.4	0.0	−11.4
3300	−1.5	0.0	−2.8	−11.1	−27.1
	−1.5	1.4	0.0	−7.0	−21.6
	−1.5	3.7	4.7	0.0	−12.3
3200	−1.5	0.0	−3.0	−12.1	−29.3
	−1.5	1.5	0.0	−7.5	−23.2
	−1.5	4.0	5.0	0.0	−13.2
3100	−1.5	0.0	−3.3	−13.1	−31.7
	−1.5	1.7	0.0	−8.1	−25.1
	−1.5	4.4	5.4	0.0	−14.2
3000	−1.5	0.0	−3.7	−14.3	−34.5
	−1.5	1.8	0.0	−8.8	−27.1
	−1.5	4.8	5.9	0.0	−15.4
2900	−1.5	0.0	−4.1	−15.6	−37.5
	−1.5	2.0	0.0	−9.5	−29.4
	−1.5	5.2	6.4	0.0	−16.7

52/53-Grain Bullets (BC = .230)

Muzzle Velocity (fps)	Muzzle	100 yards	200 yards	300 yards	400 yards
3400	−1.5	0.0	−2.6	−10.6	−26.0
	−1.5	1.3	0.0	−6.7	−20.9
	−1.5	3.5	4.5	0.0	−11.9
3300	−1.5	0.0	−2.8	−11.4	−28.1
	−1.5	1.4	0.0	−7.2	−22.4
	−1.5	3.8	4.8	0.0	−12.8
3200	−1.5	0.0	−3.1	−12.4	−30.3
	−1.5	1.6	0.0	−7.8	−24.1
	−1.5	4.1	5.2	0.0	−13.8
3100	−1.5	0.0	−3.4	−13.5	−32.9
	−1.5	1.7	0.0	−8.4	−26.0
	−1.5	4.5	5.6	0.0	−14.8
3000	−1.5	0.0	−3.8	−14.7	−35.7
	−1.5	1.9	0.0	−9.0	−28.2
	−1.5	4.9	6.1	0.0	−16.1
2900	−1.5	0.0	−4.2	−16.1	−38.8
	−1.5	2.1	0.0	−9.8	−30.5
	−1.5	5.4	6.6	0.0	−17.4

55-Grain Bullet (BC = .235)

Muzzle Velocity (fps)	Muzzle	100 yards	200 yards	300 yards	400 yards
	−1.5	0.0	−2.8	−11.3	−27.7
3300	−1.5	1.4	0.0	−7.1	−22.1
	−1.5	3.8	4.8	0.0	−12.6
	−1.5	0.0	−3.1	−12.3	−29.9
3200	−1.5	1.5	0.0	−7.7	−23.8
	−1.5	4.1	5.1	0.0	−13.5
	−1.5	0.0	−3.4	−13.4	−32.4
3100	−1.5	1.7	0.0	−8.3	−26.0
	−1.5	4.5	5.5	0.0	−14.6
	−1.5	0.0	−3.7	−14.6	−35.2
3000	−1.5	1.9	0.0	−9.0	−27.7
	−1.5	4.9	6.0	0.0	−15.8
	−1.5	0.0	−4.1	−15.9	−38.3
2900	−1.5	2.1	0.0	−9.7	−30.0
	−1.5	5.3	6.5	0.0	−17.1
	−1.5	0.0	−4.6	−17.4	−41.7
2800	−1.5	2.3	0.0	−10.6	−32.6
	−1.5	5.8	7.0	0.0	−18.6

Chapter 5

.22-250 Remington

The .22-250 Remington began life as a wildcat cartridge back in the 1930s. A number of experimenters had developed variations on this cartridge, which resulted from necking down the .250-3000 Savage to .22 caliber, but Jerry Gebby's version is basically the one that was legitimized by Remington in 1965. Gebby had named his .22-250 wildcat the Varminter and even had the name copyrighted. This is one of the finest varmint cartridges in the lineup, and it's amazing that it took until 1965 to be offered as a factory cartridge.

When Winchester redesigned the Model 70 in 1964, it dropped the .220 Swift from the line and replaced it with a new design—the .225 Winchester. This is a semi-rimmed cartridge with slightly less case capacity than the .220 Swift. It did not achieve the popularity that Winchester had hoped for. When Remington introduced the .22-250 a year later, the .225 Winchester began a slow decline that ended in 1972, when Winchester stopped chambering rifles for it.

The .22-250 is an excellent varmint cartridge that offers a high degree of accuracy and is effective on most varmint-size game out to 400 yards.

THE RUGER MODEL 77 MK II TARGET

The Ruger Model 77 MK II Target is a high-quality bolt-action target rifle with a black laminated hardwood stock. The barreled action has a pewter finish that Ruger calls Target Gray. The rifle features a heavy 26 inch stainless-steel barrel and Ruger's two-stage target trigger. The target-style stock has a wide forearm for shooting from the benchrest.

The rifling twist for the .22-250 Remington is 1:14".

The trigger is of the two-stage design and is adjustable for weight of pull. I adjusted the trigger pull on this rifle to one and a half pounds. There is no creep after the first stage is taken up, and the trigger breaks cleanly.

The scope is a variable power 6-18×40mm Nikon Buckmaster with side-focus parallax adjustment. I mounted this scope using the rings Ruger supplied.

With its 26 inch heavy barrel and wide forearm stock, the Model 77 Mark II Target, in combination with its scope and mounts, weighs slightly more than eleven pounds. Fitted with a bipod, it should make an excellent long-range varmint rifle.

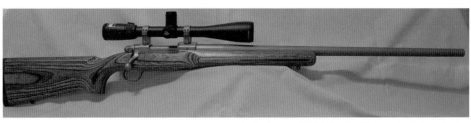

Author's Ruger Model 77 MK II Target—.22-250 Remington.

.22-250 REMINGTON FACTORY AMMO

Factory ammunition for the popular .22-250 Remington is available from just about every manufacturer, including Federal, Hornady, Nosler, Remington, and Winchester.

With its high velocity and flat trajectory, the .22-250 Remington is suitable for all varieties of varmints out to 400 yards. This cartridge may not, however, be the best choice for varmint shooting in settled areas where noise could be a factor.

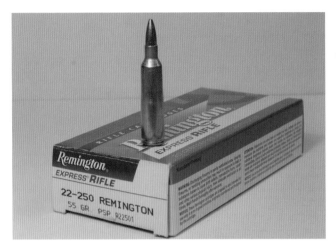

The .22-250 Remington is a popular varmint cartridge that started life as a wildcat back in the 1930s and was first offered as a factory round by Remington in 1965.

This is an accurate, flat-shooting cartridge that is effective on varmints out to 400 yards.

Federal Premium Ammunition

Bullet Weight (Grains)	Bullet Type	Velocity (fps)					Energy (ft-lbs)				
		Muzzle	100 yards	200 yards	300 yards	400 yards	Muzzle	100 yards	200 yards	300 yards	400 yards
43	Speer TNT	4000	3252	2618	2065	1590	1528	1010	654	407	241
50	Barnes Triple-Shock X	3780	3223	2732	2291	1892	1586	1153	829	582	397
55	Soft point	3650	3136	2679	2264	1888	1627	1201	876	626	435
55	Sierra GameKing	3650	3218	2827	2468	2137	1627	1265	976	744	558
60	Nosler Partition	3500	3043	2630	2253	1908	1632	1234	922	676	485

Hornady Varmint Ammunition

Bullet Weight (Grains)	Bullet Type	Velocity (fps)					Energy (ft-lbs)				
		Muzzle	100 yards	200 yards	300 yards	400 yards	Muzzle	100 yards	200 yards	300 yards	400 yards
35	NTX	4450	3709	3080	2532	2048	1539	1069	737	498	325
40	V-MAX	4150	3553	3032	2568	2148	1529	1121	816	585	410
50	V-MAX	4000	3517	3086	2694	2334	1776	1373	1057	8089	605
55	V-MAX	3680	3253	2867	2511	2183	1654	1292	1003	770	582
60	SP	3600	3195	2826	2485	2169	1726	1360	1063	823	627

Nosler Trophy Grade Varmint Ammunition

Bullet Weight (Grains)	Bullet Type	Velocity (fps)					Energy (ft-lbs)				
		Muzzle	100 yards	200 yards	300 yards	400 yards	Muzzle	100 yards	200 yards	300 yards	400 yards
35	BTLF	4200	3606	3089	2630	2213	1371	1010	741	538	381
40	BTLF	3750	3258	3820	2422	2057	1249	943	706	521	376
55	BT	3700	3295	2928	2589	2274	1672	1326	1047	819	631

Nosler Varmageddon Ammunition

Bullet Weight (Grains)	Bullet Type	Velocity (fps)					Energy (ft-lbs)				
		Muzzle	100 yards	200 yards	300 yards	400 yards	Muzzle	100 yards	200 yards	300 yards	400 yards
55	FBHP	3550	3050	2601	2195	1827	1539	1136	826	588	408
55	FBSP	3550	3136	2758	2410	2088	1539	1200	929	709	533

Remington Varmint Ammunition

Bullet Weight (Grains)	Bullet Type	Velocity (fps)					Energy (ft-lbs)				
		Muzzle	100 yards	200 yards	300 yards	400 yards	Muzzle	100 yards	200 yards	300 yards	400 yards
45	Disintegrator Varmint	4000	3293	2690	2159	1696	1598	1084	723	466	287
50	AccuTip-V	3800	3339	2925	2546	2198	1603	1283	949	720	536
50	JHP	3820	3245	2739	2286	1878	1620	1169	833	580	392

Winchester Varmint Ammunition

Bullet Weight (Grains)	Bullet Type	Velocity (fps)					Energy (ft-lbs)				
		Muzzle	100 yards	200 yards	300 yards	400 yards	Muzzle	100 yards	200 yards	300 yards	400 yards
35	Silvertip	4350	3279	3189	2711	2280	1470	1081	790	571	404
45	Jacketed HP	4000	3346	2781	2281	1837	1598	1118	773	520	337
50	Silvertip	3810	3341	2919	2536	2182	1611	1239	946	714	529
55	Silvertip	3680	3272	2900	2550	2240	1654	1307	1027	799	613

HANDLOADING THE .22-250 REMINGTON

All the current reloading manuals list data for the .22-250 Remington. In addition, Hodgdon publishes an annual reloading manual in magazine format that includes load data for the .22-250 Remington.

Barnes Reloading Manual Number 4

The Barnes manual only lists loads for the 36-, 45-, and 53-grain bullets because its .22-250 Remington test barrel had a 1:14" twist, which Barnes states was too slow for its 62- and 70-grain bullets. For each bullet weight, the firm identifies the powder that produces the most accurate loads. For example, Accurate's 2015 powder produced the most accurate loads for the 45-grain bullet, and Ramshot's TAC was the most accurate load for the Barnes 53-grain TSX FB bullet. The tests were done using a 24 inch barrel.

Hornady Handbook of Cartridge Reloading, 8th Edition

Hornady Handbook lists loads for the .22-250 Remington for bullets ranging from 40 to 80 grains, but you must observe its notes regarding rifling twists for the various bullet types. For example, the Hornady 80-grain A-MAX bullet requires a twist of 1:9" or faster.

All loads were tested in a Remington Model 700 rifle with a 26 inch barrel. Hornady states that Hodgdon's Varget powder gave excellent accuracy across the full range of Hornady bullets. It recommends the 40-grain V-MAX bullet loaded with Varget powder for prairie dog shooting.

Lyman Reloading Handbook, 49th Edition

The Lyman manual lists .22-250 Remington loads for bullet weights from 36 to 63 grains. The best accuracy for the 36-grain Barnes Varmint Grenade bullet was with Hodgdon's Varget powder. Reloder 15 yielded the best accuracy for the 45-grain SPT bullet. The best accuracy for the Hornady 40-grain V-MAX bullet was with IMR 4064 powder; for the 50-grain Sierra Blitz bullet, IMR 4895. Varget also proved to be the most accurate powder for the 52-grain A-MAX bullet. The best accuracy for the 53-grain Barnes TSX bullet and the 63-grain SMP bullet was obtained with Hodgdon's H380 powder. Vihtavuori N150 gave the best accuracy for both the 55-grain V-MAX and the 60-grain HP bullets. Lyman's test data was based on its Universal Receiver using a 24 inch barrel with a 1:14" twist.

Norma Reloading Manual Edition No. 1

While the Norma manual includes data for bullet weights of 40, 50, 52, 55, 60, and 62 grains, as a powder manufacturing company it lists only Norma powders in the load tables. For the 40-grain bullet weight, loads are listed for Norma's 201, 202, and 203-B powders. For the 50-, 52-, 55-, 60-, and 62-grain bullets, load data is given for the Norma 202 and 203-B powders.

Nosler Reloading Guide No. 6

Loads for the .22-250 Remington in the Nosler manual are listed for the Nosler 40-, 50-, 52-, 55-, 60-, 69-, 77-, and 80-grain bullets. They were tested in a rifle with a 24 inch barrel. For the 40-grain bullet, Nosler's most accurate powder was Ramshot's TAC. For the 50-, 52-, and 60-grain bullets, the most accurate powder was H380. For the 55-grain bullet, the most accurate was Big Game. Vihtavuori N540 powder proved the most accurate for the 69-grain bullet, and the Nosler 77- and 80-grain bullets liked Vihtavuori N160 the best.

Sierra 5th Edition Reloading Manual

The Sierra manual includes loads for the Sierra 40-, 45-, 50-, 52/53-, 55-, 60-, 63/65-, 69-, and 80-grain bullets. Vihtavuori N140 powder produced the best accuracy with the Sierra 40-grain bullets, and Viht N550 produced the best accuracy with the Sierra 45-grain bullets. The accuracy load for the Sierra 50-, 52-, and 53-grain bullets was obtained with Reloder 15; for the 55-grain bullets, Hodgdon's H380. The Sierra 60-grain bullet preferred Varget for the best accuracy. The test rifle was a Remington Model 700 with a 26 inch barrel and a twist of 1:14".

Speer Reloading Manual #14

The Speer manual includes .22-250 Remington loads for its 40-, 45-, 50-, 52-, 55-, and 70-grain bullets. Speer lists powders that most of the other manuals include, but does not identify any powders as producing the best accuracy. Its test firearm was a Remington Model 700 with a 24 inch barrel; it does not list the barrel's rifling twist.

The following tables list some loads from the current reloading manuals for each bullet weight from 40 to 60 grains. I consider those weights suitable for varmint shooting with the .22-250 Remington. I have not included data from the Norma manual because it lists loads only for the Norma powders. If you have a supply of these powders, I recommend that you consult the *Norma Reloading Manual*, 1st edition, for load data.

Alliant Reloder 15 Powder—40-Grain Bullet*

Manual	Minimum Charge	Muzzle Velocity	Maximum Charge	Muzzle Velocity	Barrel Length, Twist Rate
Hornady	34.3 grains	3600 fps	37.9 grains	4100 fps	26" barrel, 1:14"
Lyman	34.5 grains	3493 fps	38.0 grains	4017 fps	24" barrel, 1:14"
Nosler	33.0 grains	3431 fps	37.0 grains	3990 fps	24" barrel, 1:14"
Sierra	34.5 grains	3600 fps	37.7 grains	4000 fps	26" barrel, 1:14"
Speer	36.0 grains	3443 fps	40.0 grains	4027 fps	24" barrel

*The Barnes manual does not list a 40-grain bullet.

Alliant Reloder 15 Powder—45-Grain Bullet*

Manual	Minimum Charge	Muzzle Velocity	Maximum Charge	Muzzle Velocity	Barrel Length, Twist Rate
Barnes	35.0 grains	3644 fps	38.5 grains	4033 fps	24" barrel, 1:14"
Hornady	29.2 grains	3100 fps	34.7 grains	3600 fps	26" barrel, 1:14"
Lyman	33.6 grains	3465 fps	37.0 grains	3947 fps	24" barrel, 1:14"
Sierra	34.0 grains	3500 fps	36.7 grains	3800 fps	26" barrel, 1:14"
Speer	35.0 grains	3351 fps	39.0 grains	3897 fps	24" barrel

*The Nosler manual does not list a 45-grain bullet.

Alliant Reloder 15 Powder—50-Grain Bullet*

Manual	Minimum Charge	Muzzle Velocity	Maximum Charge	Muzzle Velocity	Barrel Length, Twist Rate
Hornady	32.1 grains	3300 fps	36.5 grains	3800 fps	26" barrel, 1:14"
Sierra	33.0 grains	3400 fps	36.0 grains	3700 fps	26" barrel, 1:14"
Speer	34.0 grains	3209 fps	38.0 grains	3736 fps	24" barrel

*The Barnes manual does not list a 50-grain bullet. The Lyman and Nosler manuals do not list RL 15 powder for the 50-grain bullet.

Alliant Reloder 15 Powder—52/53-Grain Bullets*

Manual	Minimum Charge	Muzzle Velocity	Maximum Charge	Muzzle Velocity	Barrel Length, Twist Rate
Barnes	34.5 grains	3452 fps	38.0 grains	3848 fps	24" barrel, 1:14"
Hornady	31.0 grains	3200 fps	35.8 grains	3700 fps	26" barrel, 1:14"
Lyman	32.3 grains	3239 fps	36.0 grains	3666 fps	24" barrel, 1:14"
Sierra	32.5 grains	3300 fps	35.7 grains	3700 fps	26" barrel, 1:14"
Speer	33.5 grains	3204 fps	37.5 grains	3662 fps	24" barrel

*The Nosler manual does not list RL 15 powder for the 52/53-grain bullets.

Alliant Reloder 15 Powder—55-Grain Bullet*

Manual	Minimum Charge	Muzzle Velocity	Maximum Charge	Muzzle Velocity	Barrel Length, Twist Rate
Hornady	31.0 grains	3200 fps	35.3 grains	3600 fps	26" barrel, 1:14"
Lyman	31.7 grains	3306 fps	35.5 grains	3694 fps	24" barrel, 1:14"
Sierra	32.0 grains	3300 fps	35.3 grains	3600 fps	26" barrel, 1:14"

*The Barnes manual does not list a 55-grain bullet. The Nosler and Speer manuals do not list RL 15 powder for the 55-grain bullet.

Alliant Reloder 15 Powder—60-Grain Bullet*

Manual	Minimum Charge	Muzzle Velocity	Maximum Charge	Muzzle Velocity	Barrel Length, Twist Rate
Hornady	30.4 grains	3100 fps	34.9 grains	3500 fps	26" barrel, 1:14"
Lyman	31.8 grains	3242 fps	35.0 grains	3610 fps	24" barrel, 1:14"
Nosler	30.0 grains	3220 fps	34.0 grains	3540 fps	24" barrel, 1:14"
Sierra	30.5 grains	3100 fps	33.8 grains	3400 fps	26" barrel, 1:14"

*The Barnes and Speer manuals do not list a 60-grain bullet.

Hodgdon VARGET Powder—40-Grain Bullet*

Manual	Minimum Charge	Muzzle Velocity	Maximum Charge	Muzzle Velocity	Barrel Length, Twist Rate
Hornady	33.3 grains	3600 fps	38.4 grains	4100 fps	26" barrel, 1:14"
Lyman	36.0 grains	3690 fps	40.0 grains	4130 fps	24" barrel, 1:14"
Nosler	34.0 grains	3625 fps	38.0 grains	4100 fps	24" barrel, 1:14"
Sierra	34.9 grains	3600 fps	37.3 grains	3900 fps	26" barrel, 1:14"
Speer	35.0 grains	3582 fps	39.0 grains	4090 fps	24" barrel

*The Barnes manual does not list a 40-grain bullet.

Hodgdon VARGET Powder—45-Grain Bullet*

Manual	Minimum Charge	Muzzle Velocity	Maximum Charge	Muzzle Velocity	Barrel Length, Twist Rate
Barnes	35.0 grains	3653 fps	38.5 grains	4023 fps	24" barrel, 1:14"
Hornady	29.6 grains	3100 fps	34.2 grains	3600 fps	26" barrel, 1:14"
Lyman	36.0 grains	3538 fps	39.5 grains	3982 fps	24" barrel, 1:14"
Sierra	34.4 grains	3500 fps	36.5 grains	3800 fps	26" barrel, 1:14"
Speer	33.5 grains	3345 fps	37.5 grains	3881 fps	24" barrel

*The Nosler manual does not list a 45-grain bullet.

Hodgdon VARGET Powder—50-Grain Bullet*

Manual	Minimum Charge	Muzzle Velocity	Maximum Charge	Muzzle Velocity	Barrel Length, Twist Rate
Hornady	31.8 grains	3300 fps	36.4 grains	3800 fps	26" barrel, 1:14"
Nosler	32.0 grains	3415 fps	36.0 grains	3794 fps	24" barrel, 1:14"
Sierra	33.0 grains	3400 fps	36.0 grains	3700 fps	26" barrel, 1:14"
Speer	32.5 grains	3283 fps	36.5 grains	3796 fps	24" barrel

*The Barnes manual does not list a 50-grain bullet. The Lyman manual does not list Varget powder for the 50-grain bullet.

Hodgdon VARGET Powder—52/53-Grain Bullets

Manual	Minimum Charge	Muzzle Velocity	Maximum Charge	Muzzle Velocity	Barrel Length, Twist Rate
Barnes	34.0 grains	3434 fps	37.5 grains	3805 fps	24" barrel, 1:14"
Hornady	30.7 grains	3200 fps	35.7 grains	3700 fps	26" barrel, 1:14"
Lyman	33.5 grains	3367 fps	38.0 grains	3764 fps	24" barrel, 1:14"
Nosler	32.0 grains	3415 fps	36.0 grains	3794 fps	24" barrel, 1:14"
Sierra	32.3 grains	3300 fps	35.3 grains	3600 fps	26" barrel, 1:14"
Speer	32.0 grains	3338 fps	36.0 grains	3706 fps	24" barrel

Hodgdon VARGET Powder—55-Grain Bullet*

Manual	Minimum Charge	Muzzle Velocity	Maximum Charge	Muzzle Velocity	Barrel Length, Twist Rate
Hornady	30.8 grains	3200 fps	34.6 grains	3600 fps	26" barrel, 1:14"
Lyman	34.0 grains	3325 fps	37.0 grains	3696 fps	24" barrel, 1:14"
Nosler	31.0 grains	3273 fps	35.0 grains	3635 fps	24" barrel, 1:14"
Sierra	32.1 grains	3300 fps	36.1 grains	3700 fps	26" barrel, 1:14"
Speer	32.0 grains	3260 fps	36.0 grains	3655 fps	24" barrel

*The Barnes manual does not list a 55-grain bullet.

Hodgdon VARGET Powder—60-Grain Bullet*

Manual	Minimum Charge	Muzzle Velocity	Maximum Charge	Muzzle Velocity	Barrel Length, Twist Rate
Hornady	29.5 grains	3100 fps	34.1 grains	3500 fps	26" barrel, 1:14"
Lyman	32.5 grains	3165 fps	36.0 grains	3493 fps	24" barrel, 1:14"
Nosler	30.0 grains	3270 fps	34.0 grains	3525 fps	24" barrel, 1:14"
Sierra	30.6 grains	3100 fps	32.8 grains	3300 fps	26" barrel, 1:14"

*The Barnes and Speer manuals do not list a 60-grain bullet.

IMR 4895 Powder—40-Grain Bullet*

Manual	Minimum Charge	Muzzle Velocity	Maximum Charge	Muzzle Velocity	Barrel Length, Twist Rate
Hornady	32.9 grains	3600 fps	36.1 grains	4000 fps	26" barrel, 1:14"
Lyman	34.2 grains	3402 fps	37.0 grains	3919 fps	24" barrel, 1:14"
Nosler	32.0 grains	3395 fps	36.0 grains	3961 fps	24" barrel, 1:14"
Sierra	34.1 grains	3600 fps	36.8 grains	4000 fps	26" barrel, 1:14"

*The Barnes manual does not list a 40-grain bullet. The Hornady manual lists H4895 powder, which is similar to IMR 4895 powder but not identical in burning characteristics. The Speer manual does not list IMR 4895 powder for the 40-grain bullet.

IMR 4895 Powder—45-Grain Bullet*

Manual	Minimum Charge	Muzzle Velocity	Maximum Charge	Muzzle Velocity	Barrel Length, Twist Rate
Barnes	34.5 grains	3626 fps	38.0 grains	4035 fps	24" barrel, 1:14"
Hornady	27.5 grains	3100 fps	32.5 grains	3600 fps	26" barrel, 1:14"
Lyman	32.5 grains	3353 fps	36.5 grains	3901 fps	24" barrel, 1:14"
Sierra	33.5 grains	3500 fps	36.5 grains	3900 fps	26" barrel, 1:14"
Speer	32.0 grains	3209 fps	36.0 grains	3647 fps	24" barrel

*The Hornady manual lists H4895 powder, which is similar to IMR 4895 powder but not identical in burning characteristics. The Nosler manual does not list a 45-grain bullet.

IMR 4895 Powder—50-Grain Bullet*

Manual	Minimum Charge	Muzzle Velocity	Maximum Charge	Muzzle Velocity	Barrel Length, Twist Rate
Hornady	30.0 grains	3300 fps	35.4 grains	3800 fps	26" barrel, 1:14"
Lyman	33.5 grains	3230 fps	37.0 grains	3704 fps	24" barrel, 1:14"
Nosler	30.0 grains	3352 fps	34.0 grains	3802 fps	24" barrel, 1:14"
Sierra	32.7 grains	3400 fps	35.9 grains	3800 fps	26" barrel, 1:14"
Speer	31.5 grains	3116 fps	35.5 grains	3561 fps	24" barrel

*The Barnes manual does not list a 50-grain bullet. The Hornady manual lists H4895 powder, which is similar to IMR 4895 powder but not identical in burning characteristics.

IMR 4895 Powder—52/53-Grain Bullets*

Manual	Minimum Charge	Muzzle Velocity	Maximum Charge	Muzzle Velocity	Barrel Length, Twist Rate
Barnes	33.0 grains	3365 fps	36.5 grains	3769 fps	24" barrel, 1:14"
Hornady	29.5 grains	3200 fps	33.8 grains	3600 fps	26" barrel, 1:14"
Lyman	32.6 grains	3157 fps	36.2 grains	3604 fps	24" barrel, 1:14"
Nosler	30.0 grains	3352 fps	34.0 grains	3802 fps	24" barrel, 1:14"
Sierra	31.7 grains	3300 fps	35.3 grains	3700 fps	26" barrel, 1:14"
Speer	31.0 grains	3121 fps	35.0 grains	3526 fps	24" barrel

*The Hornady manual lists H4895 powder, which is similar to IMR 4895 powder but not identical in burning characteristics.

IMR 4895 Powder—55-Grain Bullet*

Manual	Minimum Charge	Muzzle Velocity	Maximum Charge	Muzzle Velocity	Barrel Length, Twist Rate
Lyman	32.0 grains	3152 fps	35.5 grains	3576 fps	24" barrel, 1:14"
Nosler	30.0 grains	3112 fps	34.0 grains	3602 fps	24" barrel, 1:14"
Sierra	32.0 grains	3300 fps	34.9 grains	3600 fps	26" barrel, 1:14"
Speer	31.0 grains	2993 fps	35.0 grains	3421 fps	24" barrel

*The Barnes manual does not list a 55-grain bullet. The Hornady manual does not list IMR 4895 powder for the 55-grain bullet.

IMR 4895 Powder—60-Grain Bullet*

Manual	Minimum Charge	Muzzle Velocity	Maximum Charge	Muzzle Velocity	Barrel Length, Twist Rate
Lyman	33.0 grains	3141 fps	36.0 grains	3581 fps	24" barrel, 1:14"
Nosler	29.0 grains	3164 fps	33.0 grains	3540 fps	24" barrel, 1:14"
Sierra	30.7 grains	3100 fps	34.3 grains	3500 fps	26" barrel, 1:14"

*The Barnes and Speer manuals do not list a 60-grain bullet. The Hornady manual does not list IMR 4895 powder for the 60-grain bullet.

IMR 4064 Powder—40-Grain Bullet*

Manual	Minimum Charge	Muzzle Velocity	Maximum Charge	Muzzle Velocity	Barrel Length, Twist Rate
Hornady	33.7 grains	3600 fps	37.0 grains	4100 fps	26" barrel, 1:14"
Lyman	34.7 grains	3365 fps	38.5 grains	3920 fps	24" barrel, 1:14"
Sierra	33.5 grains	3600 fps	38.0 grains	4100 fps	26" barrel, 1:14"
Speer	34.0 grains	3390 fps	38.0 grains	3830 fps	24" barrel

*The Barnes manual does not list a 40-grain bullet. The Nosler manual does not list IMR 4064 powder for the 40-grain bullet.

IMR 4064 Powder—45-Grain Bullet*

Manual	Minimum Charge	Muzzle Velocity	Maximum Charge	Muzzle Velocity	Barrel Length, Twist Rate
Hornady	30.2 grains	3100 fps	34.4 grains	3600 fps	26" barrel, 1:14"
Lyman	33.0 grains	3373 fps	37.5 grains	3945 fps	24" barrel, 1:14"
Sierra	34.0 grains	3500 fps	36.7 grains	3900 fps	26" barrel, 1:14"
Speer	33.5 grains	3207 fps	37.5 grains	3665 fps	24" barrel

*The Barnes manual does not list IMR 4064 powder for the 45-grain bullet. The Nosler manual does not list a 45-grain bullet.

IMR 4064 Powder—50-Grain Bullet*

Manual	Minimum Charge	Muzzle Velocity	Maximum Charge	Muzzle Velocity	Barrel Length, Twist Rate
Hornady	31.8 grains	3300 fps	35.9 grains	3800 fps	26" barrel, 1:14"
Lyman	32.0 grains	3210 fps	37.0 grains	3854 fps	24" barrel, 1:14"
Nosler	30.5 grains	3250 fps	34.5 grains	3690 fps	24" barrel, 1:14"
Sierra	32.8 grains	3400 fps	36.2 grains	3800 fps	26" barrel, 1:14"
Speer	33.0 grains	3136 fps	37.0 grains	3625 fps	24" barrel

*The Barnes manual does not list a 50-grain bullet.

IMR 4064 Powder—52/53-Grain Bullets*

Manual	Minimum Charge	Muzzle Velocity	Maximum Charge	Muzzle Velocity	Barrel Length, Twist Rate
Hornady	31.3 grains	3200 fps	35.5 grains	3700 fps	26" barrel, 1:14"
Lyman	32.3 grains	3123 fps	36.0 grains	3657 fps	24" barrel, 1:14"
Nosler	30.5 grains	3250 fps	34.5 grains	3690 fps	24" barrel, 1:14"
Sierra	31.8 grains	3300 fps	35.5 grains	3700 fps	26" barrel, 1:14"
Speer	32.5 grains	3064 fps	36.5 grains	3563 fps	24" barrel

*The Barnes and Lyman manuals do not list IMR 4064 powder for the 53-grain bullet.

IMR 4064 Powder—55-Grain Bullet*

Manual	Minimum Charge	Muzzle Velocity	Maximum Charge	Muzzle Velocity	Barrel Length, Twist Rate
Hornady	31.3 grains	3200 fps	34.9 grains	3600 fps	26" barrel, 1:14"
Lyman	32.0 grains	3221 fps	35.5 grains	3634 fps	24" barrel, 1:14"
Nosler	30.5 grains	3211 fps	34.5 grains	3603 fps	24" barrel, 1:14"
Sierra	32.6 grains	3300 fps	35.7 grains	3700 fps	26" barrel, 1:14"
Speer	32.0 grains	2999 fps	36.0 grains	3467 fps	24" barrel

*The Barnes manual does not list a 55-grain bullet.

IMR 4064 Powder—60-Grain Bullet*

Manual	Minimum Charge	Muzzle Velocity	Maximum Charge	Muzzle Velocity	Barrel Length, Twist Rate
Hornady	29.9 grains	3100 fps	34.4 grains	3500 fps	26" barrel, 1:14"
Lyman	31.0 grains	3128 fps	35.5 grains	3589 fps	24" barrel, 1:14"
Nosler	29.0 grains	3145 fps	33.0 grains	3500 fps	24" barrel, 1:14"
Sierra	30.6 grains	3100 fps	35.6 grains	3600 fps	26" barrel, 1:14"

*The Barnes and Speer manuals do not list a 60-grain bullet.

RANGE TESTS

On the day I performed the range tests for the .22-250 Remington, it was sunny, there was a slight breeze from about 12 o'clock, and the temperature was in the high 80s. For the factory ammo test, I picked Remington's 50-grain jacketed hollow point ammunition, the results of which can be found on the next page.

Group 1 measured 1.21" center to center, with four of the shots in 0.89", and group 2 measured 1.2". I consider this reasonable accuracy for factory ammunition.

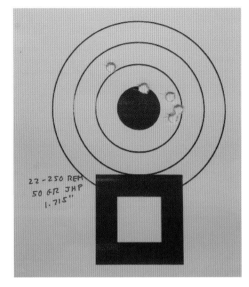

.22-250 Remington—Factory Ammo Group 1.

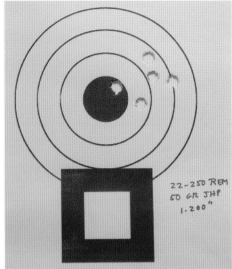

.22-250 Remington—Factory Ammo Group 2.

2877-01-2875-
2863-02-2861-
2930-03-2926-
2871-04-2869-
2888-05-2886-
2960-06-2908-

06-2926-+
06-2861--
06-0065-T
06-2887-M
06-0024-$

The chronograph data for Remington's factory ammunition indicates an average velocity (M) of 3794 fps and a standard deviation ($) of 26 fps.

This is in close agreement with Remington's data for the 50-grain bullet in the .22-250 Remington.

The Oehler chronograph measured an average velocity of 3794 fps for the Remington factory ammo, which compares quite favorably with Remington's data for the 50-grain bullet.

My handload (Sierra 52-grain hollow point boat tail bullet, 33 grains of IMR 4064 powder, and CCI 200 primer) produced the following five-shot groups.

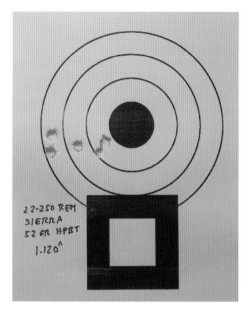

.22-250 Remington—Handload Group 1.

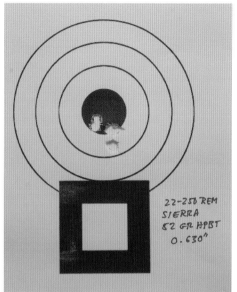

.22-250 Remington—Handload Group 2.

```
3581-01-3568-
3490-02-3478-
3502-03-3491-
3571-04-3558-
3565-05-3557-
3587-06-3568-
3623-07-3601-
3616-08-3598-
3590-09-3573-
3623-10-3603-

--------

10-3603-+
10-3478--
10-0125-T
10-3559-M
10-0043-$

--------
```

For my .22-250 handload, the chronograph indicates an average velocity (M) of 3271 fps and a standard deviation (S) of 21 fps.

This reading is in agreement with that published by the various reloading manuals.

The first group measured 1.12", and the second group measured 0.63". No doubt, a few more groups would provide a better indication of the accuracy for this load.

The chronograph measured an average velocity of 3271 fps. This is in the ballpark of the data in the reloading manuals.

I consider this load to be a little on the mild side for the .22-250 Remington and plan to increase the charge incrementally to possibly 35 grains, which should yield a velocity closer to 3600 fps. If accuracy improves—or at least does not degrade—and there are no indications of pressure problems, I will go with the increased charge. As indicated by handload group 2, the .22-250 Remington and Ruger Model 77 MK II Target combination show potential for being fine long-range varmint rifles out to 400 yards.

TRAJECTORY TABLES

The following trajectory tables were developed using the Handloads.com ballistic calculator. The tables are based on the line of sight (LOS) being 1.5 inches above the line of fire (LOF). All tabular data is expressed in inches.

40-Grain Bullet (BC = .200)

Muzzle Velocity (fps)	Muzzle	100 yards	200 yards	300 yards	400 yards
4100	−1.5	0.0	−1.4	−6.8	−17.7
	−1.5	0.7	0.0	−4.7	−15.0
	−1.5	2.3	3.1	0.0	−8.7
4000	−1.5	0.0	−1.5	−7.3	−18.9
	−1.5	0.8	0.0	−5.0	−15.9
	−1.5	2.4	3.3	0.0	−9.2
3900	−1.5	0.0	−1.7	−7.8	−20.2
	−1.5	0.9	0.0	−5.3	−16.9
	−1.5	2.6	3.5	0.0	−9.8
3800	−1.5	0.0	−1.9	−8.4	−21.7
	−1.5	0.9	0.0	−5.6	−17.9
	−1.5	2.8	3.8	0.0	−10.4
3700	−1.5	0.0	−2.1	−9.1	−23.2
	−1.5	1.0	0.0	−6.0	−19.1
	−1.5	3.0	4.0	0.0	−11.1
3600	−1.5	0.0	−2.3	−9.8	−25.0
	−1.5	1.1	0.0	−6.4	−20.4
	−1.5	3.3	4.3	0.0	−11.9
3500	−1.5	0.0	−2.5	−10.6	−26.8
	−1.5	1.3	0.0	−6.9	−21.8
	−1.5	3.5	4.6	0.0	−12.7
3400	−1.5	0.0	−2.7	−11.5	−28.8
	−1.5	1.4	0.0	−7.4	−23.4
	−1.5	3.8	4.9	0.0	−13.6

45-Grain Bullet (BC = .202)

Muzzle Velocity (fps)	Muzzle	100 yards	200 yards	300 yards	400 yards
	−1.5	0.0	−1.5	−7.2	−18.8
4000	−1.5	0.8	0.0	−4.9	−15.7
	−1.5	2.4	3.3	0.0	−9.2
	−1.5	0.0	−1.7	−7.8	−20.1
3900	−1.5	0.8	0.0	−5.3	−16.7
	−1.5	2.6	3.5	0.0	−9.7
	−1.5	0.0	−1.9	−8.4	−21.5
3800	−1.5	0.9	0.0	−5.6	−17.8
	−1.5	2.8	3.7	0.0	−10.3
	−1.5	0.0	−2.1	−9.0	−23.0
3700	−1.5	1.0	0.0	−6.0	−18.9
	−1.5	3.0	4.0	0.0	−11.0
	−1.5	0.0	−2.3	−9.8	−24.7
3600	−1.5	1.1	0.0	−6.4	−20.2
	−1.5	3.4	4.3	0.0	−11.7
	−1.5	0.0	−2.5	−10.6	−26.6
3500	−1.5	1.2	0.0	−6.8	−21.7
	−1.5	3.5	4.6	0.0	−12.6
	−1.5	0.0	−2.7	−11.4	−26.7
3400	−1.5	1.4	0.0	−7.3	−23.2
	−1.5	3.8	4.9	0.0	−13.5
	−1.5	0.0	−3.0	−12.4	−31.0
3300	−1.5	1.5	0.0	−7.9	−25.0
	−1.5	4.1	5.3	0.0	−14.5

50-Grain Bullet (BC = .242)

Muzzle Velocity (fps)	Muzzle	100 yards	200 yards	300 yards	400 yards
	−1.5	0.0	−1.7	−7.5	−18.8
3800	−1.5	0.8	0.0	−5.0	−15.4
	−1.5	2.5	3.3	0.0	−8.8
	−1.5	0.0	−1.8	−8.1	−20.1
3700	−1.5	0.9	0.0	−5.3	−16.5
	−1.5	2.7	3.5	0.0	−9.4
	−1.5	0.0	−2.0	−8.7	−21.6
3600	−1.5	1.0	0.0	−5.7	−17.5
	−1.5	2.9	3.6	0.0	−10.0
	−1.5	0.0	−2.3	−9.5	−23.4
3500	−1.5	1.1	0.0	−6.1	−18.7
	−1.5	3.2	4.1	0.0	−10.7
	−1.5	0.0	−2.5	−10.2	−25.1
3400	−1.5	1.2	0.0	−6.5	−20.1
	−1.5	3.4	4.3	0.0	−11.4
	−1.5	0.0	−2.7	−11.1	−27.0
3300	−1.5	1.4	0.0	−7.0	−21.5
	−1.5	3.7	4.7	0.0	−12.2
	−1.5	0.0	−3.0	−12.1	−29.2
3200	−1.5	1.5	0.0	−7.5	−23.2
	−1.5	4.0	5.0	0.0	−13.1
	−1.5	0.0	−3.3	−13.1	−31.7
3100	−1.5	1.7	0.0	−8.1	−25.0
	−1.5	4.4	5.4	0.0	−14.2

55-Grain Bullet (BC = .235)

Muzzle Velocity (fps)	Muzzle	100 yards	200 yards	300 yards	400 yards
	−1.5	0.0	−1.9	−8.2	−20.6
3700	−1.5	0.9	0.0	−5.4	−16.8
	−1.5	2.7	3.6	0.0	−9.6
	−1.5	0.0	−2.1	−8.9	−22.1
3600	−1.5	1.0	0.0	−5.8	−18.0
	−1.5	3.0	3.9	0.0	−10.3
	−1.5	0.0	−2.3	−9.6	−23.8
3500	−1.5	1.2	0.0	−6.2	−19.2
	−1.5	3.2	4.1	0.0	−10.9
	−1.5	0.0	−2.5	−10.4	−25.6
3400	−1.5	1.3	0.0	−6.6	−20.6
	−1.5	3.5	4.4	0.0	−11.7
	−1.5	0.0	−2.8	−11.3	−27.7
3300	−1.5	1.4	0.0	−7.1	−22.1
	−1.5	3.8	4.8	0.0	−12.6
	−1.5	0.0	−3.1	−12.3	−29.9
3200	−1.5	1.5	0.0	−7.7	−23.8
	−1.5	4.1	5.1	0.0	−13.5
	−1.5	0.0	−3.4	−13.4	−32.4
3100	−1.5	1.7	0.0	−8.3	−23.0
	−1.5	4.5	5.5	0.0	−14.6

60-Grain Bullet (BC = .265)

Muzzle Velocity (fps)	Muzzle	100 yards	200 yards	300 yards	400 yards
	−1.5	0.0	−2.0	−8.4	−20.5
3600	−1.5	1.0	0.0	−5.4	−16.6
	−1.5	2.8	3.6	0.0	−9.4
	−1.5	0.0	−2.2	−9.0	−22.0
3500	−1.5	1.1	0.0	−5.8	−17.7
	−1.5	3.0	3.9	0.0	−10.0
	−1.5	0.0	−2.4	−9.8	−23.7
3400	−1.5	1.2	0.0	−6.2	−19.0
	−1.5	3.3	4.1	0.0	−10.7
	−1.5	0.0	−2.6	−10.6	−25.6
3300	−1.5	1.3	0.0	−6.7	−20.3
	−1.5	3.5	4.5	0.0	−11.4
	−1.5	0.0	−2.9	−11.5	−27.7
3200	−1.5	1.5	0.0	−7.2	−21.9
	−1.5	3.9	4.8	0.0	−12.3
	−1.5	0.0	−3.2	−12.6	−30.0
3100	−1.5	1.6	0.0	−7.7	−23.6
	−1.5	4.2	5.2	0.0	−13.2

Chapter 6

.220 Swift

The .220 Swift was developed by Winchester in 1935 and introduced in the firm's Model 54 bolt-action center-fire rifle. It's based on the semi-rimmed 6mm Lee Navy cartridge. In my opinion, the .220 Swift remains the king of varmint cartridges. The Swift was initially tried on everything from varmints to big game, but is best restricted to use as a varmint cartridge. It gained a reputation early on as a barrel burner, because it was loaded hot and the barrel metallurgy back then was not up to the pressure and heat that this cartridge generated. When Winchester replaced the Model 54 with the Model 70 in 1937, it used a stainless-steel barrel for the Swift chambering.

Because of its undeserved reputation, the Swift eventually fell out of popularity. And when Winchester redesigned the Model 70 in 1964, it dropped the Swift and replaced it with the .225 Winchester. But thanks to Ruger and Sako, the Swift was revived in the early 1970s. With advances in barrel metallurgy and an understanding by reloaders that it still performs great at velocities slightly less than the magic 4000 fps, the Swift is alive and well today.

Offering excellent accuracy and a flat trajectory, this cartridge is ideally suited as a varmint cartridge for ranges of 400 yards and beyond. Unfortunately, the only factory rifle currently chambered for this cartridge is the Remington Model 700. Ironically, Winchester has yet to resurrect this round and, in fact, chambers the latest version of the Model 70 for the .22-250 Remington.

THE RUGER MODEL 77V

The Ruger Model 77V, my first real varmint rifle and my first Ruger bolt action, has a heavy 26 inch barrel and an adjustable trigger that I set to a crisp pull of one and a half pounds. This model is generally referred to as the tang safety version and preceded the later MK II version, which has a side-mounted safety. My particular model was made in 1976 and has the words "MADE IN THE 200TH YEAR OF AMERICAN LIBERTY" engraved on the side of the barrel. This is often referred to as the Liberty model.

The closest model to my 77V that Ruger makes today is the MK II Target. Unfortunately, Ruger no longer chambers any of its rifles for the Swift.

The rifling twist for the .220 Swift is 1:14".

The scope I installed on this rifle is a Leupold M8 with a fixed power of 12X. It has an adjustable objective for parallax correction. The scope is mounted using the rings Ruger supplied.

With its 26 inch heavy barrel and varmint stock, the Model 77V, in combination with its scope and mounts, weighs close to ten pounds.

Author's Ruger Model 77V—.220 Swift.

.220 SWIFT FACTORY AMMO

Factory ammunition for the .220 Swift is available from Federal, Hornady, Remington, and Winchester. Federal only offers a load for the 40-grain bullet. Both Remington and Winchester only offer a load for the 50-grain pointed soft point bullet. Hornady offers the best selection with loads for 50-, 55-, and 60-grain bullets. The .220 Swift is a better performer when handloaded.

With its high velocity and flat trajectory, the .220 Swift is suitable for varmints, such as prairie dogs and woodchucks, to 400 yards and beyond. This cartridge is an excellent choice for long-range varmint shooting in rural areas where noise is not a factor.

The .220 Swift, introduced by Winchester in 1935, is still a great varmint cartridge. It's deadly on prairie dogs and woodchucks at ranges of 400 yards and beyond.

Federal Premium Ammunition

Bullet Weight (Grains)	Bullet Type	Velocity (fps)					Energy (ft-lbs)				
		Muzzle	100 yards	200 yards	300 yards	400 yards	Muzzle	100 yards	200 yards	300 yards	400 yards
40	Nosler Ballistic Tip	4250	3694	3204	2766	2367	1604	1212	912	679	498

Hornady Varmint Express Ammunition

Bullet Weight (Grains)	Bullet Type	Velocity (fps)					Energy (ft-lbs)				
		Muzzle	100 yards	200 yards	300 yards	400 yards	Muzzle	100 yards	200 yards	300 yards	400 yards
50	Hornady V-MAX	3850	3384	2695	2583	2232	1645	1271	976	741	553
55	Hornady V-MAX	3680	3253	2867	2511	2183	1654	1292	1003	770	582
60	HP	3600	3195	2826	2485	2169	1726	1360	1063	823	627

Remington Rifle Ammunition

Bullet Weight (Grains)	Bullet Type	Velocity (fps)					Energy (ft-lbs)				
		Muzzle	100 yards	200 yards	300 yards	400 yards	Muzzle	100 yards	200 yards	300 yards	400 yards
50	PSP	3780	3158	2617	2135	1710	1586	1107	760	506	325

Winchester Super-X Ammunition

Bullet Weight (Grains)	Bullet Type	Velocity (fps)					Energy (ft-lbs)				
		Muzzle	100 yards	200 yards	300 yards	400 yards	Muzzle	100 yards	200 yards	300 yards	400 yards
50	PSP	3870	3310	2816	2373	1972	1663	1226	881	625	432

HANDLOADING THE .220 SWIFT

The handloader has a definite advantage over factory ammo users when it comes to the .220 Swift. The factory bullet selections are somewhat limited, but the handloader can choose bullets ranging from 40 to 80 grains. Bullets heavier than 60 grains, however, should be used in rifles having a twist faster than 1:14". I will only include loads for bullets up to 60 grains in the following tables, as I believe this is the upper limit for what I consider a varmint load for the Swift. I am sure some will disagree with me.

Barnes Reloading Manual Number 4

The Barnes manual only lists loads for the 36-, 45-, and 53-grain bullets, and it recommends a twist of 1:12" or faster to stabilize its 45-grain Banded Solid Spitzer and 53-grain TSX bullets. Its .220 Swift test barrel had a 1:14" twist. For each bullet weight, Barnes identifies the powder that produces the most accurate loads. For example, Hodgdon's H380 powder produced the most accurate loads for the 45-grain bullet, and IMR 4007 SSC was the most accurate load for the Barnes 53-grain TSX FB bullet. The tests were performed using a 24 inch barrel.

Hornady Handbook of Cartridge Reloading, 8th Edition

The *Hornady Handbook* lists loads for the Hornady 40-, 45-, 50-, 52/53-, 55-, and 60-grain bullets. All loads were tested in a Ruger Model 77 Mark II rifle with a 26 inch barrel. Hornady's most accurate loads were with Vihtavuori N140, H4895, and Varget powders in combination with its 55- and 60-grain bullets.

Lyman Reloading Handbook, 49th Edition

The Lyman manual lists .220 Swift loads for bullet weights from 40 to 70 grains. The best accuracy for the 40-grain jacketed SP bullet was with IMR 3031 powder. Vihtavuori N150 powder gave the best accuracy for both the 45-grain SPT and the 50-grain Sierra Blitz bullet. Vihtavuori N160 proved to be the most accurate powder for the 55- and 60-grain jacketed bullets. IMR 4350 was the accurate powder for both the 63- and 70-grain bullets. Lyman's test data was based on its Universal Receiver using a 24 inch barrel with a 1:14" twist.

Norma Reloading Manual Edition No. 1

While the Norma manual includes data for bullet weights of 40, 50, 52, 55, 60, and 62 grains, as a powder manufacturing company it lists only Norma powders in the load tables.

Norma 202 and 203-B powders are listed as the powders of choice for all bullet weights.

Nosler Reloading Guide No. 6

Loads for the .220 Swift are listed in the Nosler manual for the Nosler 40-, 50-, 52-, 55-, and 60-grain bullets. They were tested using a rifle with a 26 inch barrel and twist of 1:14". For the 40-grain bullet, Nosler's most accurate powder was H380. For the 50- and 52-grain bullets, the most accurate powder was AA2520. For the 55-grain bullet, the most accurate powder was IMR 4831. And for the 60-grain Nosler Partition Spitzer, IMR 4350 proved the most accurate powder.

Sierra 5th Edition Reloading Manual

The Sierra manual includes loads for the Sierra 40-, 45-, 50-, 52-, 53-, 55-, 60-, 63-, 65-, 69-, and 80-grain bullets. Its best accuracy for the 40-, 52/53-, and 55-grain bullets was obtained using Reloder 15. Vihtavuori N140 produced the best accuracy for the 45-grain SPT bullet. The best 50-grain bullet accuracy was obtained with IMR 4320 powder. Hodgdon's H380 gave the best accuracy for the 60-grain bullet, and AA2700 was the accurate powder for the 63- and 65-grain bullets. Sierra notes that a twist of 1:10" or faster is required for the 63- and

65-grain bullets. The Sierra MatchKing 69- and 80-grain bullets are not recommended for hunting applications. The test rifle for the Sierra load tables was a Savage 12VSS with a 26 inch barrel.

Speer Reloading Manual #14

The Speer manual includes .220 Swift loads for its 40-, 45-, 50-, 52-, 55-, and 70-grain bullets. Speer lists powders that most of the other manuals do, but does not identify any powders as producing the best accuracy. Its test firearm was a Ruger Model 77V with a 26 inch barrel. It does not list this barrel's rifling twist, but in all probability it was 1:14".

The following tables list some loads from the current reloading manuals for each bullet weight from 40 to 60 grains. I consider these weights suitable for varmint shooting with the .220 Swift. I have not included data from the Norma manual because it only lists loads for Norma powders. If you have a supply of these powders, I recommend that you consult the *Norma Reloading Manual*, 1st edition, for load data.

For the .220 Swift handload, I'm going to use the Hornady 60-grain hollow point bullet, 33 grains of IMR 4064 powder, the CCI 200 primer, and Winchester brass.

IMR 3031 Powder—40-Grain Bullet*

Manual	Minimum Charge	Muzzle Velocity	Maximum Charge	Muzzle Velocity	Barrel Length, Twist Rate
Hornady	33.3 grains	3800 fps	38.3 grains	4300 fps	26" barrel, 1:14"
Lyman	35.0 grains	3906 fps	39.0 grains	4385 fps	26" barrel, 1:14"
Nosler	32.0 grains	3364 fps	36.0 grains	4005 fps	26" barrel, 1:14"
Sierra	35.8 grains	3800 fps	38.2 grains	4100 fps	26" barrel, 1:14"
Speer	34.5 grains	3509 fps	38.5 grains	3878 fps	26" barrel

*The Barnes manual does not list a 40-grain bullet.

IMR 3031 Powder—45-Grain Bullet*

Manual	Minimum Charge	Muzzle Velocity	Maximum Charge	Muzzle Velocity	Barrel Length, Twist Rate
Lyman	34.0 grains	3717 fps	38.5 grains	4219 fps	26" barrel, 1:14"
Sierra	35.1 grains	3700 fps	38.4 grains	4100 fps	26" barrel, 1:14"
Speer	33.5 grains	3332 fps	37.5 grains	3723 fps	26" barrel

*The Barnes and Hornady manuals do not list IMR 3031 powder for the 45-grain bullet. The Nosler manual does not list loads for the 45-grain bullet.

IMR 3031 Powder—50-Grain Bullet*

Manual	Minimum Charge	Muzzle Velocity	Maximum Charge	Muzzle Velocity	Barrel Length, Twist Rate
Lyman	34.0 grains	3650 fps	38.0 grains	4065 fps	26" barrel, 1:14"
Sierra	34.5 grains	3600 fps	37.1 grains	3900 fps	26" barrel, 1:14"
Speer	33.0 grains	3282 fps	37.0 grains	3607 fps	26" barrel

*The Barnes manual does not list a 50-grain bullet. The Hornady and Nosler manuals do not list IMR 3031 powder for the 50-grain bullet.

IMR 3031 Powder—52/53-Grain Bullets*

Manual	Minimum Charge	Muzzle Velocity	Maximum Charge	Muzzle Velocity	Barrel Length, Twist Rate
Sierra	33.5 grains	3500 fps	36.5 grains	3800 fps	26" barrel, 1:14"
Speer	32.5 grains	3254 fps	36.5 grains	3576 fps	26" barrel

*The Barnes, Hornady, and Nosler manuals do not list IMR 3031 powder for the 52/53-grain bullets. The Lyman manual does not list 52/53-grain bullets.

IMR 3031 Powder—55-Grain Bullet*

Manual	Minimum Charge	Muzzle Velocity	Maximum Charge	Muzzle Velocity	Barrel Length, Twist Rate
Lyman	33.0 grains	3509 fps	37.0 grains	3921 fps	26" barrel, 1:14"
Sierra	32.8 grains	3400 fps	36.8 grains	3800 fps	26" barrel, 1:14"
Speer	32.0 grains	3201 fps	36.0 grains	3506 fps	26" barrel

*The Barnes manual does not list a 55-grain bullet. The Hornady and Nosler manuals do not list IMR 3031 powder for the 55-grain bullet.

IMR 3031 Powder—60-Grain Bullet*

Manual	Minimum Charge	Muzzle Velocity	Maximum Charge	Muzzle Velocity	Barrel Length, Twist Rate
Sierra	30.8 grains	3100 fps	33.5 grains	3300 fps	26" barrel, 1:14"

*The Barnes and Speer manuals do not list a 60-grain bullet. The Hornady, Lyman, Nosler, and Speer manuals do not list IMR 3031 powder for the 60-grain bullet.

Hodgdon VARGET Powder—40-Grain Bullet*

Manual	Minimum Charge	Muzzle Velocity	Maximum Charge	Muzzle Velocity	Barrel Length, Twist Rate
Hornady	36.8 grains	3800 fps	40.9 grains	4200 fps	26" barrel, 1:14"
Nosler	35.0 grains	3579 fps	39.0 grains	4067 fps	26" barrel, 1:14"
Sierra	38.2 grains	3800 fps	40.0 grains	4000 fps	26" barrel, 1:14"

*The Barnes manual does not list a 40-grain bullet. The Lyman and Speer manuals do not list Varget powder for the 40-grain bullet.

Hodgdon VARGET Powder—45-Grain Bullet*

Manual	Minimum Charge	Muzzle Velocity	Maximum Charge	Muzzle Velocity	Barrel Length, Twist Rate
Hornady	36.8 grains	3800 fps	40.9 grains	4200 fps	26" barrel, 1:14"
Sierra	37.6 grains	3700 fps	39.6 grains	3900 fps	26" barrel, 1:14"

*The Barnes, Lyman, and Speer manuals do not list Varget powder for the 45-grain bullet. The Nosler manual does not list a 45-grain bullet.

Hodgdon VARGET Powder—50-Grain Bullet*

Manual	Minimum Charge	Muzzle Velocity	Maximum Charge	Muzzle Velocity	Barrel Length, Twist Rate
Hornady	33.2 grains	3400 fps	38.7 grains	3900 fps	26" barrel, 1:14"
Nosler	32.0 grains	3409 fps	36.0 grains	3787 fps	26" barrel, 1:14"
Sierra	37.0 grains	3600 fps	39.0 grains	3800 fps	26" barrel, 1:14"

*The Barnes manual does not list a 50-grain bullet. The Lyman and Speer manuals do not list Varget powder for the 50-grain bullet.

Hodgdon VARGET Powder—52/53-Grain Bullets*

Manual	Minimum Charge	Muzzle Velocity	Maximum Charge	Muzzle Velocity	Barrel Length, Twist Rate
Hornady	32.2 grains	3300 fps	37.0 grains	3700 fps	26" barrel, 1:14"
Nosler	32.0 grains	3409 fps	36.0 grains	3787 fps	26" barrel, 1:14"
Sierra	36.6 grains	3500 fps	38.2 grains	3700 fps	26" barrel, 1:14"

*The Barnes and Speer manuals do not list Varget powder for the 52/53-grain bullets. The Lyman manual does not list 52/53-grain bullets.

Hodgdon VARGET Powder—55-Grain Bullet*

Manual	Minimum Charge	Muzzle Velocity	Maximum Charge	Muzzle Velocity	Barrel Length, Twist Rate
Hornady	31.9 grains	3300 fps	36.6 grains	3700 fps	26" barrel, 1:14"
Nosler	31.0 grains	3243 fps	35.0 grains	3587 fps	26" barrel, 1:14"
Sierra	34.2 grains	3400 fps	37.8 grains	3700 fps	26" barrel, 1:14"

*The Barnes manual does not list a 55-grain bullet. The Lyman and Speer manuals do not list Varget powder for the 55-grain bullet.

Hodgdon VARGET Powder—60-Grain Bullet*

Manual	Minimum Charge	Muzzle Velocity	Maximum Charge	Muzzle Velocity	Barrel Length, Twist Rate
Hornady	30.3 grains	3100 fps	34.1 grains	3400 fps	26" barrel, 1:14"
Lyman	32.5 grains	3288 fps	36.0 grains	3507 fps	26" barrel, 1:14"
Sierra	32.3 grains	3100 fps	36.7 grains	3600 fps	26" barrel, 1:14"

*The Barnes and Speer manuals do not list a 60-grain bullet. The Nosler manual does not list Varget powder for the 60-grain bullet.

IMR 4064 Powder—40-Grain Bullet*

Manual	Minimum Charge	Muzzle Velocity	Maximum Charge	Muzzle Velocity	Barrel Length, Twist Rate
Hornady	36.5 grains	3800 fps	40.2 grains	4200 fps	26" barrel, 1:14"
Lyman	37.0 grains	3891 fps	41.0 grains	4347 fps	26" barrel, 1:14"
Nosler	34.0 grains	3441 fps	38.0 grains	3949 fps	26" barrel, 1:14"
Sierra	37.9 grains	3800 fps	40.6 grains	4200 fps	26" barrel, 1:14"
Speer	35.0 grains	3380 fps	39.0 grains	3715 fps	26" barrel

*The Barnes manual does not list a 40-grain bullet.

IMR 4064 Powder—45-Grain Bullet*

Manual	Minimum Charge	Muzzle Velocity	Maximum Charge	Muzzle Velocity	Barrel Length, Twist Rate
Hornady	29.8 grains	3100 fps	34.9 grains	3600 fps	26" barrel, 1:14"
Lyman	36.0 grains	3626 fps	40.5 grains	4184 fps	26" barrel, 1:14"
Sierra	37.2 grains	3700 fps	39.4 grains	4000 fps	26" barrel, 1:14"
Speer	33.5 grains	3284 fps	37.5 grains	3653 fps	26" barrel

*The Barnes manual does not list IMR 4064 powder for the 45-grain bullet. The Nosler manual does not list a 45-grain bullet.

IMR 4064 Powder—50-Grain Bullet*

Manual	Minimum Charge	Muzzle Velocity	Maximum Charge	Muzzle Velocity	Barrel Length, Twist Rate
Hornady	33.1 grains	3400 fps	38.2 grains	3900 fps	26" barrel, 1:14"
Lyman	36.0 grains	3650 fps	40.0 grains	4081 fps	26" barrel, 1:14"
Sierra	36.4 grains	3600 fps	39.9 grains	4000 fps	26" barrel, 1:14"
Speer	34.0 grains	3208 fps	38.0 grains	3564 fps	26" barrel, 1:14"

*The Barnes manual does not list a 50-grain bullet. The Nosler manual does not list IMR 4064 powder for the 50-grain bullet.

IMR 4064 Powder—52/53-Grain Bullets*

Manual	Minimum Charge	Muzzle Velocity	Maximum Charge	Muzzle Velocity	Barrel Length, Twist Rate
Hornady	32.7 grains	3300 fps	37.5 grains	3800 fps	26" barrel, 1:14"
Sierra	35.0 grains	3500 fps	38.7 grains	3900 fps	26" barrel, 1:14"

*The Barnes, Nosler, and Speer manuals do not list IMR 4064 powder for the 53-grain bullet. The Lyman manual does not list 52/53-grain bullets.

IMR 4064 Powder—55-Grain Bullet*

Manual	Minimum Charge	Muzzle Velocity	Maximum Charge	Muzzle Velocity	Barrel Length, Twist Rate
Hornady	31.8 grains	3300 fps	36.4 grains	3700 fps	26" barrel, 1:14"
Lyman	35.0 grains	3472 fps	39.0 grains	3906 fps	26" barrel, 1:14"
Nosler	34.0 grains	3299 fps	38.0 grains	3767 fps	26" barrel, 1:14"
Sierra	34.0 grains	3400 fps	38.0 grains	3800 fps	26" barrel, 1:14"

*The Barnes manual does not list a 55-grain bullet. The Speer manual does not list IMR 4064 powder for the 55-grain bullet.

IMR 4064 Powder—60-Grain Bullet*

Manual	Minimum Charge	Muzzle Velocity	Maximum Charge	Muzzle Velocity	Barrel Length, Twist Rate
Hornady	30.1 grains	3100 fps	34.2 grains	3500 fps	26" barrel, 1:14"
Lyman	33.3 grains	3296 fps	37.0 grains	3572 fps	26" barrel, 1:14"
Sierra	32.1 grains	3100 fps	34.3 grains	3300 fps	26" barrel, 1:14"

*The Barnes and Speer manuals do not list a 60-grain bullet. The Nosler manual does not list IMR 4064 powder for its 60-grain bullet.

Alliant Reloder 15 Powder—40-Grain Bullet*

Manual	Minimum Charge	Muzzle Velocity	Maximum Charge	Muzzle Velocity	Barrel Length, Twist Rate
Hornady	37.0 grains	3800 fps	40.8 grains	4300 fps	26" barrel, 1:14"
Nosler	35.0 grains	3618 fps	39.0 grains	4165 fps	26" barrel, 1:14"
Sierra	37.8 grains	3800 fps	40.5 grains	4100 fps	26" barrel, 1:14"
Speer	37.0 grains	3580 fps	41.0 grains	3996 fps	26" barrel

*The Barnes manual does not list a 40-grain bullet. The Lyman manual does not list RL 15 for the 40-grain bullet.

Alliant Reloder 15 Powder—45-Grain Bullet*

Manual	Minimum Charge	Muzzle Velocity	Maximum Charge	Muzzle Velocity	Barrel Length, Twist Rate
Barnes	37.5 grains	3824 fps	40.5 grains	4105 fps	24" barrel, 1:14"
Hornady	29.8 grains	3100 fps	35.9 grains	3600 fps	26" barrel, 1:14"
Lyman	36.5 grains	3708 fps	40.5 grains	4121 fps	26" barrel, 1:14"
Sierra	37.2 grains	3700 fps	39.9 grains	4000 fps	26" barrel, 1:14"
Speer	37.5 grains	3537 fps	41.5 grains	4010 fps	26" barrel

*The Nosler manual does not list loads for a 45-grain bullet.

Alliant Reloder 15 Powder—50-Grain Bullet*

Manual	Minimum Charge	Muzzle Velocity	Maximum Charge	Muzzle Velocity	Barrel Length, Twist Rate
Hornady	33.4 grains	3400 fps	38.2 grains	3800 fps	26" barrel, 1:14"
Nosler	33.0 grains	3343 fps	37.0 grains	3754 fps	26" barrel, 1:14"
Sierra	36.4 grains	3600 fps	39.4 grains	3900 fps	26" barrel, 1:14"
Speer	36.0 grains	3388 fps	40.0 grains	3782 fps	26" barrel

*The Barnes manual does not list a 50-grain bullet. The Lyman manual does not list RL 15 powder for the 50-grain bullet.

Alliant Reloder 15 Powder—52/53-Grain Bullets*

Manual	Minimum Charge	Muzzle Velocity	Maximum Charge	Muzzle Velocity	Barrel Length, Twist Rate
Barnes	36.0 grains	3564 fps	39.0 grains	3835 fps	24" barrel, 1:14"
Hornady	32.4 grains	3300 fps	38.0 grains	3700 fps	26" barrel, 1:14"
Nosler	33.0 grains	3343 fps	37.0 grains	3754 fps	26" barrel, 1:14"
Sierra	35.8 grains	3500 fps	38.0 grains	3700 fps	26" barrel, 1:14"
Speer	35.5 grains	3353 fps	39.5 grains	3742 fps	26" barrel

*The Lyman manual does not list 52/53-grain bullets.

Alliant Reloder 15 Powder—55-Grain Bullet*

Manual	Minimum Charge	Muzzle Velocity	Maximum Charge	Muzzle Velocity	Barrel Length, Twist Rate
Hornady	31.7 grains	3300 fps	36.3 grains	3700 fps	26" barrel, 1:14"
Nosler	33.0 grains	3468 fps	37.0 grains	3662 fps	26" barrel, 1:14"
Sierra	34.0 grains	3400 fps	37.9 grains	3700 fps	26" barrel, 1:14"
Speer	35.0 grains	3276 fps	39.0 grains	3656 fps	26" barrel

*The Barnes manual does not list a 55-grain bullet. The Lyman manual does not list RL 15 powder for the 55-grain bullet.

Alliant Reloder 15 Powder—60-Grain Bullet*

Manual	Minimum Charge	Muzzle Velocity	Maximum Charge	Muzzle Velocity	Barrel Length, Twist Rate
Hornady	30.1 grains	3100 fps	35.3 grains	3500 fps	26" barrel, 1:14"
Nosler	31.5 grains	3320 fps	35.5 grains	3598 fps	26" barrel, 1:14"
Sierra	32.0 grains	3100 fps	36.4 grains	3500 fps	26" barrel, 1:14"

*The Barnes and Speer manuals do not list a 60-grain bullet. The Lyman manual does not list RL 15 powder for the 60-grain bullet.

IMR 4350 Powder—40-Grain Bullet*

Manual	Minimum Charge	Muzzle Velocity	Maximum Charge	Muzzle Velocity	Barrel Length, Twist Rate
Lyman	39.0 grains	3546 fps	43.0 grains	3968 fps	26" barrel, 1:14"
Speer	41.0 grains	3424 fps	45.0 grains	3883 fps	26" barrel

*The Barnes manual does not list a 40-grain bullet. The Hornady, Nosler, and Sierra manuals do not list IMR 4350 powder for the 40-grain bullet.

IMR 4350 Powder—45-Grain Bullet*

Manual	Minimum Charge	Muzzle Velocity	Maximum Charge	Muzzle Velocity	Barrel Length, Twist Rate
Lyman	39.0 grains	3521 fps	43.0 grains	3861 fps	26" barrel, 1:14"
Speer	40.5 grains	3066 fps	44.5 grains	3476 fps	26" barrel

*The Barnes, Hornady, and Sierra manuals do not list IMR 4350 powder for the 45-grain bullet. The Nosler manual does not list a 45-grain bullet.

IMR 4350 Powder—50-Grain Bullet*

Manual	Minimum Charge	Muzzle Velocity	Maximum Charge	Muzzle Velocity	Barrel Length, Twist Rate
Lyman	39.0 grains	3509 fps	43.0 grains	3921 fps	26" barrel, 1:14"
Nosler	38.0 grains	3478 fps	42.0 grains	3888 fps	26" barrel, 1:14"
Sierra	41.9 grains	3600 fps	43.6 grains	3800 fps	26" barrel, 1:14"
Speer	40.0 grains	3265 fps	44.0 grains	3703 fps	26" barrel

*The Barnes manual does not list a 50-grain bullet. The Hornady manual does not list IMR 4350 powder for the 50-grain bullet. The Sierra manual lists XMR 4350 powder, which is produced by Accurate Arms and does not have the same burning rate as IMR 4350.

IMR 4350 Powder—52/53-Grain Bullets*

Manual	Minimum Charge	Muzzle Velocity	Maximum Charge	Muzzle Velocity	Barrel Length, Twist Rate
Nosler	38.0 grains	3478 fps	42.0 grains	3888 fps	26" barrel, 1:14"
Sierra	40.6 grains	3500 fps	42.2 grains	3700 fps	26" barrel, 1:14"
Speer	39.0 grains	3253 fps	43.0 grains	3688 fps	26" barrel

*The Barnes and Hornady manuals do not list IMR 4350 powder for the 53-grain bullet. The Lyman manual does not list 52/53-grain bullets. The Sierra manual lists XMR 4350 powder, which is produced by Accurate Arms and does not have the same burning rate as IRM 4350.

IMR 4350 Powder—55-Grain Bullet*

Manual	Minimum Charge	Muzzle Velocity	Maximum Charge	Muzzle Velocity	Barrel Length, Twist Rate
Hornady	37.1 grains	3300 fps	42.2 grains	3800 fps	26" barrel, 1:14"
Lyman	38.0 grains	3356 fps	42.5 grains	3787 fps	26" barrel, 1:14"
Sierra	39.1 grains	3400 fps	42.4 grains	3700 fps	26" barrel, 1:14"
Speer	39.0 grains	3167 fps	43.0 grains	3591 fps	26" barrel

*The Barnes manual does not list a 55-grain bullet. The Nosler manual does not list IMR 4350 powder for the 55-grain bullet.

IMR 4350 Powder—60-Grain Bullet*

Manual	Minimum Charge	Muzzle Velocity	Maximum Charge	Muzzle Velocity	Barrel Length, Twist Rate
Hornady	34.8 grains	3100 fps	40.1 grains	3600 fps	26" barrel, 1:14"
Lyman	37.8 grains	3236 fps	42.0 grains	3559 fps	26" barrel, 1:14"
Nosler	35.5 grains	3330 fps	39.5 grains	3630 fps	26" barrel, 1:14"
Sierra	36.8 grains	3100 fps	38.9 grains	3300 fps	26" barrel, 1:14"

*The Barnes and Speer manuals do not list a 60-grain bullet.

RANGE TESTS

The weather on the day I conducted the .220 Swift range tests was partly sunny with a variable wind from 6 o'clock. The temperature was in the mid-70s. For the factory test, I used the Remington 50-grain pointed soft point, the results of which can be found on the next page.

Group 1 measured 1.2" center to center, with four of the shots in 0.78", and group 2 measured 1.16" center to center, with four of the shots in 0.63". I consider this good accuracy for factory ammunition.

The Oehler chronograph measured an average velocity of 3685 fps for the Remington factory ammo, which is about 100 fps lower than Remington's data for the 50-grain bullet.

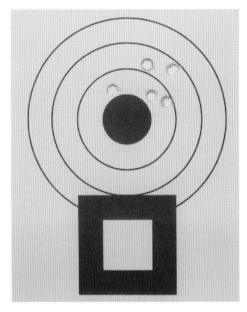

.220 Swift—Factory Ammo Group 1.

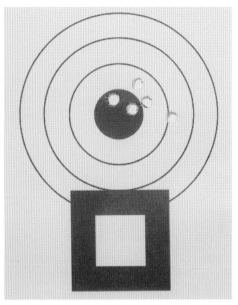

.220 Swift—Factory Ammo Group 2.

```
2877-01-2875-
2863-02-2861-
2930-03-2926-
2871-04-2869-
2888-05-2886-
2960-06-2908-

------
      06-2926-+
      06-2861--
      06-0065-T
      06-2887-M
      06-0024-$
------
```

The chronograph data for Remington's 50-grain factory ammo indicates an average velocity (M) of 3685 fps and a standard deviation (S) of 32 fps.

This average velocity is about 100 fps lower than Remington's data for its 50-grain bullet in the .220 Swift.

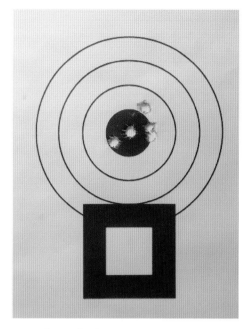

.220 Swift—Handload Group 1.

.220 Swift—Handload Group 2.

My handload—Hornady 60-grain hollow point bullet, 33 grains of IMR 4064 powder, and WRA primer—produced the following five-shot groups.

The first group measured 0.95" with four shots in 0.58", and the second group measured 1.1" with the upper four shots in 0.6". The bottom shot in the second group was my last shot—naturally! I'm not making excuses, but when I extracted that case from the chamber, it felt a little hard coming out. So take your pick: Either I got nervous about getting the fifth shot in the group, or something was different about that particular round.

The chronograph, the printout of which can be found on the next page, measured an average velocity of 3182 fps, which is in agreement with the data in the reloading manuals. This velocity is a little on the low side, so I think I will carefully try increasing the powder charge to approach a muzzle velocity closer to 3500 fps. Hopefully I can, at the same time, improve the accuracy. I believe this rifle is capable of better than 1 MOA with the 60-grain bullet. Part of the enjoyment of reloading is to safely pursue that goal.

Both the factory ammo and my handloads demonstrate that the .220 Swift remains a great varmint cartridge. However, the only factory rifle available at this time is the Remington Model 700 Varmint SF. Just as I would like to see Remington bring back the 6mm Remington in its Model 700, I wish that Winchester would reintroduce the Swift in its Model 70.

```
3581-01-3568-
3490-02-3478-
3502-03-3491-
3571-04-3558-
3565-05-3557-
3587-06-3568-
3623-07-3601-
3616-08-3598-
3590-09-3573-
3623-10-3603-
---------
10-3603-+
10-3478--
10-0125-T
10-3559-M
10-0043-$
```

For my .220 Swift handload, the chronograph indicates an average velocity (M) of 3182 fps and a standard deviation ($) of 15 fps. This low a standard deviation indicates good consistency.

This average velocity is in agreement with that published by the various reloading manuals.

TRAJECTORY TABLES

The following trajectory tables were developed using the Handloads.com ballistic calculator. The tables are based on the line of sight (LOS) being 1.5 inches above the line of fire (LOF). All tabular data is expressed in inches.

40-Grain Bullet (BC = .200)

Muzzle Velocity (fps)	Muzzle	100 yards	200 yards	300 yards	400 yards
4300	−1.5	0.0	−1.1	−5.9	−15.6
	−1.5	0.6	0.0	−4.2	−13.4
	−1.5	2.0	2.8	0.0	−7.8
4200	−1.5	0.0	−1.3	−6.3	−16.6
	−1.5	0.6	0.0	−4.4	−14.2
	−1.5	2.1	3.0	0.0	−8.3
4100	−1.5	0.0	−1.4	−6.8	−17.7
	−1.5	0.7	0.0	−4.7	−15.0
	−1.5	2.3	3.1	0.0	−8.7
4000	−1.5	0.0	−1.5	−7.3	−18.9
	−1.5	0.8	0.0	−5.0	−15.9
	−1.5	2.4	3.3	0.0	−9.2
3900	−1.5	0.0	−1.7	−7.8	−20.2
	−1.5	0.9	0.0	−5.3	−16.9
	−1.5	2.6	3.5	0.0	−9.8
3800	−1.5	0.0	−1.9	−8.4	−21.7
	−1.5	0.9	0.0	−5.6	−17.9
	−1.5	2.8	3.8	0.0	−10.4
3700	−1.5	0.0	−2.1	−9.1	−23.2
	−1.5	1.0	0.0	−6.0	−19.1
	−1.5	3.0	4.0	0.0	−11.1
3600	−1.5	0.0	−2.3	−9.8	−25.0
	−1.5	1.1	0.0	−6.4	−20.4
	−1.5	3.3	4.3	0.0	−11.9
3500	−1.5	0.0	−2.5	−10.6	−26.8
	−1.5	1.3	0.0	−6.9	−21.8
	−1.5	3.5	4.6	0.0	−12.7

45-Grain Bullet (BC = .202)

Muzzle Velocity (fps)	Muzzle	100 yards	200 yards	300 yards	400 yards
	−1.5	0.0	−1.2	−6.3	−16.5
4200	−1.5	0.6	0.0	−4.4	−14.0
	−1.5	2.1	2.9	0.0	−8.2
	−1.5	0.0	−1.4	−6.7	−17.6
4100	−1.5	0.7	0.0	−4.7	−14.9
	−1.5	2.2	3.1	0.0	−8.7
	−1.5	0.0	−1.5	−7.2	−18.8
4000	−1.5	0.8	0.0	−4.9	−15.7
	−1.5	2.4	3.3	0.0	−9.2
	−1.5	0.0	−1.7	−7.8	−20.1
3900	−1.5	0.8	0.0	−5.3	−16.7
	−1.5	2.6	3.5	0.0	−9.7
	−1.5	0.0	−1.9	−8.4	−21.5
3800	−1.5	0.9	0.0	−5.6	−17.8
	−1.5	2.8	3.7	0.0	−10.3
	−1.5	0.0	−2.1	−9.0	−23.0
3700	−1.5	1.0	0.0	−6.0	−18.9
	−1.5	3.0	4.0	0.0	−11.0
	−1.5	0.0	−2.3	−9.8	−24.7
3600	−1.5	1.1	0.0	−6.4	−20.2
	−1.5	3.4	4.3	0.0	−11.7
	−1.5	0.0	−2.5	−10.6	−26.6
3500	−1.5	1.2	0.0	−6.8	−21.7
	−1.5	3.5	4.6	0.0	−12.6
	−1.5	0.0	−2.7	−11.4	−26.7
3400	−1.5	1.4	0.0	−7.3	−23.2
	−1.5	3.8	4.9	0.0	−13.5
	−1.5	0.0	−3.0	−12.4	−31.0
3300	−1.5	1.5	0.0	−7.9	−25.0
	−1.5	4.1	5.3	0.0	−14.5

50-Grain Bullet (BC = .242)

Muzzle Velocity (fps)	Muzzle	100 yards	200 yards	300 yards	400 yards
4000	−1.5	0.0	−1.4	−6.4	−16.4
	−1.5	0.7	0.0	−4.4	−13.7
	−1.5	2.2	2.9	0.0	−7.9
3900	−1.5	0.0	−1.5	−7.0	−17.6
	−1.5	0.8	0.0	−4.7	−14.6
	−1.5	2.3	3.1	0.0	−8.3
3800	−1.5	0.0	−1.7	−7.5	−18.8
	−1.5	0.8	0.0	−5.0	−15.4
	−1.5	2.5	3.3	0.0	−8.8
3700	−1.5	0.0	−1.8	−8.1	−20.1
	−1.5	0.9	0.0	−5.3	−16.5
	−1.5	2.7	3.5	0.0	−9.4
3600	−1.5	0.0	−2.0	−8.7	−21.6
	−1.5	1.0	0.0	−5.7	−17.5
	−1.5	2.9	3.6	0.0	−10.0
3500	−1.5	0.0	−2.3	−9.5	−23.4
	−1.5	1.1	0.0	−6.1	−18.7
	−1.5	3.2	4.1	0.0	−10.7
3400	−1.5	0.0	−2.5	−10.2	−25.1
	−1.5	1.2	0.0	−6.5	−20.1
	−1.5	3.4	4.3	0.0	−11.4
3300	−1.5	0.0	−2.7	−11.1	−27.0
	−1.5	1.4	0.0	−7.0	−21.5
	−1.5	3.7	4.7	0.0	−12.2
3200	−1.5	0.0	−3.0	−12.1	−29.2
	−1.5	1.5	0.0	−7.5	−23.2
	−1.5	4.0	5.0	0.0	−13.1

55-Grain Bullet (BC = .235)

Muzzle Velocity (fps)	Muzzle	100 yards	200 yards	300 yards	400 yards
	−1.5	0.0	−1.9	−8.2	−20.6
3700	−1.5	0.9	0.0	−5.4	−16.8
	−1.5	2.7	3.6	0.0	−9.6
	−1.5	0.0	−2.1	−8.9	−22.1
3600	−1.5	1.0	0.0	−5.8	−18.0
	−1.5	3.0	3.9	0.0	−10.3
	−1.5	0.0	−2.3	−9.6	−23.8
3500	−1.5	1.2	0.0	−6.2	−19.2
	−1.5	3.2	4.1	0.0	−10.9
	−1.5	0.0	−2.5	−10.4	−25.6
3400	−1.5	1.3	0.0	−6.6	−20.6
	−1.5	3.5	4.4	0.0	−11.7
	−1.5	0.0	−2.8	−11.3	−27.7
3300	−1.5	1.4	0.0	−7.1	−22.1
	−1.5	3.8	4.8	0.0	−12.6
	−1.5	0.0	−3.1	−12.3	−29.9
3200	−1.5	1.5	0.0	−7.7	−23.8
	−1.5	4.1	5.1	0.0	−13.5
	−1.5	0.0	−3.4	−13.4	−32.4
3100	−1.5	1.7	0.0	−8.3	−23.0
	−1.5	4.5	5.5	0.0	−14.6

60-Grain Bullet (BC = .265)

Muzzle Velocity (fps)	Muzzle	100 yards	200 yards	300 yards	400 yards
	−1.5	0.0	−2.0	−8.4	−20.5
3600	−1.5	1.0	0.0	−5.4	−16.6
	−1.5	2.8	3.6	0.0	−9.4
	−1.5	0.0	−2.2	−9.0	−22.0
3500	−1.5	1.1	0.0	−5.8	−17.7
	−1.5	3.0	3.9	0.0	−10.0
	−1.5	0.0	−2.4	−9.8	−23.7
3400	−1.5	1.2	0.0	−6.2	−19.0
	−1.5	3.3	4.1	0.0	−10.7
	−1.5	0.0	−2.6	−10.6	−25.6
3300	−1.5	1.3	0.0	−6.7	−20.3
	−1.5	3.5	4.5	0.0	−11.4
	−1.5	0.0	−2.9	−11.5	−27.7
3200	−1.5	1.5	0.0	−7.2	−21.9
	−1.5	3.9	4.8	0.0	−12.3
	−1.5	0.0	−3.2	−12.6	−30.0
3100	−1.5	1.6	0.0	−7.7	−23.6
	−1.5	4.2	5.2	0.0	−13.2

Chapter 7

.243 Winchester

The .243 Winchester was announced by Winchester in 1955. This cartridge was designed to be dual purpose—used to hunt both varmints and medium-size game. Basically, it's the .308 Winchester necked down to 6mm. Because Winchester considered the .243 Winchester a dual-purpose cartridge, it opted for a rifling twist of 1:10". This allows the cartridge to handle both the lighter 60- to 80-grain bullets for varmints and the 100- to 105-grain bullets for deer and antelope. It quickly gained a following, and is popular to this day.

Credit for the initial development of the .243 Winchester goes to Warren Page who, at the time, was the shooting editor for *Field & Stream* magazine. Warren named his wildcat version the 240 Page Pooper. The .243 Winchester is accurate and has even become popular as a competitive match cartridge. With a twist of 1:7 or 1:8" and a 105- or 107-grain match bullet, this cartridge is capable of delivering good long-range accuracy, as evidenced by its use in target competition.

THE REMINGTON MODEL 700 CDL

The Remington Model 700 CDL (Classic Deluxe) is a fine example of classic rifle design. When chambered for the .243 Winchester, it's ideally suited as a walking-around varmint and medium-game rifle. The barrel is a 24 inch sporter with a twist of $1:9\frac{1}{8}$". The American walnut stock has a satin finish and hand-cut checkering. The bolt is jeweled, and the trigger is adjustable for weight of pull. I set the trigger pull to about two pounds. I also free floated the barrel. Remington typically beds its barrels with a slight upward pressure near the fore-end. My experience, even with light sporter barrels, is that free floating works best.

The scope is a Leupold VX-2 3-9×50mm with $\frac{1}{4}$ MOA windage and elevation adjustments and is mounted in Leupold high rings so the 50mm objective clears the barrel.

The weight of the rifle, in combination with the scope and rings, is slightly less than eight and a half pounds.

Because this book is about varmint rifles and cartridges, I am limiting both factory ammo and handload information for the .243 Winchester to that which is applicable to varmint shooting.

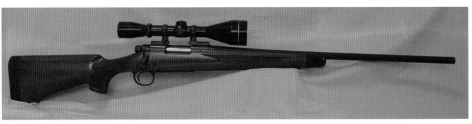

Author's Remington Model 700 CDL—.243 Winchester.

.243 WINCHESTER FACTORY AMMO

Factory ammunition for the popular .243 Winchester is available from most manufacturers, including Barnes, Federal, Hornady, Nosler, Remington, and Winchester.

The .243 Winchester was developed as a dual-purpose cartridge. With lightweight bullets from 55 to 80 grains, it's an excellent varmint round. When used with heavier 85- to 100-grain bullets, this cartridge is well-suited for medium-size game, such as deer and antelope.

When loaded with a match bullet like the Sierra 107-grain HPBT MatchKing, the .243 Winchester is also a good competitive match cartridge.

Barnes Vor-Tx Ammunition

Bullet Weight (Grains)	Bullet Type	Velocity (fps)					Energy (ft-lbs)				
		Muzzle	100 yards	200 yards	300 yards	400 yards	Muzzle	100 yards	200 yards	300 yards	400 yards
80	TTSX	3350	3042	2755	2486	2232	1994	1644	1349	1098	885

Federal V-Shok Ammunition

Bullet Weight (Grains)	Bullet Type	Velocity (fps)					Energy (ft-lbs)				
		Muzzle	100 yards	200 yards	300 yards	400 yards	Muzzle	100 yards	200 yards	300 yards	400 yards
55	Nosler Ballistic Tip	3850	3438	3064	2721	2402	1810	1444	1147	904	704
70	Nosler Ballistic Tip	3450	3113	2802	2511	2238	1850	1507	1220	980	778

Hornady Superformance Varmint Ammunition

Bullet Weight (Grains)	Bullet Type	Velocity (fps)					Energy (ft-lbs)				
		Muzzle	100 yards	200 yards	300 yards	400 yards	Muzzle	100 yards	200 yards	300 yards	400 yards
58	Hornady V-MAX	3925	3465	3051	2674	2327	1984	1546	1199	921	697

Nosler Varmageddon Ammunition

Bullet Weight (Grains)	Bullet Type	Velocity (fps)					Energy (ft-lbs)				
		Muzzle	100 yards	200 yards	300 yards	400 yards	Muzzle	100 yards	200 yards	300 yards	400 yards
55	FBHP	3800	3226	2722	2269	1863	1763	1271	905	629	424
55	FBSP	3800	3356	2955	2588	2249	1763	1375	1066	818	618

Remington Premier Ammunition

Bullet Weight (Grains)	Bullet Type	Velocity (fps)					Energy (ft-lbs)				
		Muzzle	100 yards	200 yards	300 yards	400 yards	Muzzle	100 yards	200 yards	300 yards	400 yards
75	AccuTip-V	3375	3065	2775	2504	2248	1897	1564	1282	1064	842

Winchester Supreme Ammunition

Bullet Weight (Grains)	Bullet Type	Velocity (fps)					Energy (ft-lbs)				
		Muzzle	100 yards	200 yards	300 yards	400 yards	Muzzle	100 yards	200 yards	300 yards	400 yards
55	Ballistic Silvertip	3910	3493	3114	2766	2444	1867	1489	1184	934	729
80	Super-X	3350	2955	2594	2259	1951	1993	1551	1195	907	676

HANDLOADING THE .243 WINCHESTER

All the current reloading manuals list data for the .243 Winchester. In addition, Hodgdon publishes an annual reloading manual in magazine format that includes load data for the .243 Winchester.

Barnes Reloading Manual Number 4

The Barnes manual lists loads for its 62-, 75-, and 85-grain bullets. For each bullet weight, Barnes identifies the powder that produces the most accurate loads. Alliant's Reloder 19 produced the most accurate loads for the 62-grain bullet, and Ramshot's Hunter powder was the most accurate load for the Barnes 85-grain TSX FB bullet.

Hornady Handbook of Cartridge Reloading, 8th Edition

Hornady includes loads for its 58-, 65-, 70-, 75-, 80-, 85/87-, 95/100-, and 105-grain bullets. Vihtavuori N140, IMR 4064, and Viht N160 powders performed well in Hornady's testing of the .243 Winchester. The company recommends a twist rate of 1:9" or faster for its 105-grain A-MAX bullet. For the purpose of developing loads for shooting varmints, we will only consider loads for bullet weights of 58 to 80 grains.

Lyman Reloading Handbook, 49th Edition

The Lyman manual lists .243 Winchester loads for bullet weights from 58 to 105 grains. For developing varmint loads, we will consider the load data for the 58-, 60-, 65-, 70-, 75-, and

80-grain bullets. Lyman's best accuracy for the 58-, 60-, and 65-grain bullets was obtained with IMR 4350 powder. Varget was the most accurate powder for the 70- and 75-grain bullets. For the 80-grain bullet, Lyman's best load was with AA2520 powder.

Norma Reloading Manual Edition No. 1

The Norma manual includes data for bullet weights of 80, 95, and 100 grains. However, as a powder manufacturing company, it lists only Norma powders in the load tables. For all bullet weights, load data is given for the Norma 204 and MRP powders. In addition, Norma also lists MRP-2 powder for the 95- and 100-grain bullets. MRP-2 is a slightly slower-burning version of MRP powder.

Nosler Reloading Guide No. 6

Nosler lists loads for its 55-, 70-, 80-, 85-, 90-, and 100-grain 6mm bullets. The most accurate powder for the Nosler 55-grain bullet was Hodgdon's H414. For the Nosler 70-grain bullet, Varget powder proved the most accurate. For the 80-grain bullet, it was Hodgdon's H380. And for the Nosler 85/90-grain bullets, 44.5 grains of IMR 4831 powder gave the best accuracy. Lastly, the most accurate powder tested for the Nosler 95/100-grain bullets was Vihtavuori N-560.

Sierra 5th Edition Reloading Manual

Sierra includes load tables for its 55-, 60-, 70-, 75-, 80-, 85-, 90-, 100-, and 107-grain bullets; the 107-grain HPBT MatchKing is for competition. We will only consider the loads for the 55- to 80-grain bullets as they are applicable to varmint shooting.

Sierra's accuracy load for its 55- and 60-grain bullets was with 37.6 grains of Hodgdon's Benchmark powder; for hunting, 43 grains of Varget. The best accuracy for the Sierra 70- and 75-grain bullets was obtained using Hodgdon's H322 powder. The accuracy load for the 80-grain bullet was 37.3 grains of Vihtavuori N140 powder. The best hunting load for this bullet weight was 38 grains of IMR 4064.

Speer Reloading Manual #14

The Speer manual includes .243 Winchester loads for its 70-, 75-, 80-, 85-, 90-, 100-, and 105-grain bullets. Speer lists many of the powders that most of the other manuals include, but does not identify any powders as producing the best accuracy. Also, the Speer manual does not list the twist rate for the .243 Winchester test firearm barrel.

The following tables list some loads from the current reloading manuals for each bullet weight from 55 to 80 grains. I consider these weights suitable for varmint shooting with the .243 Winchester. I have not included data from the Norma manual because it lists only loads for the Norma powders. If you intend to use any of those powders, I recommend you consult the *Norma Reloading Manual*, 1st edition, for load data.

For the .243 Winchester, I am going to try the following load: Sierra 75-grain hollow point bullet, 39 grains of Varget powder, and the CCI 200 primer.

IMR 4895 Powder—55-Grain Bullet*

Manual	Minimum Charge	Muzzle Velocity	Maximum Charge	Muzzle Velocity	Barrel Length, Twist Rate
Nosler	40.5 grains	3535 fps	44.5 grains	3935 fps	24" barrel, 1:10"
Sierra	39.7 grains	3300 fps	40.8 grains	3400 fps	22" barrel, 1:9$\frac{1}{8}$"

*Only the Nosler and Sierra manuals list loads for the 55-grain bullet.

IMR 4895 Powder—58/60/62-Grain Bullets*

Manual	Minimum Charge	Muzzle Velocity	Maximum Charge	Muzzle Velocity	Barrel Length, Twist Rate
Hornady	35.9 grains	3300 fps	40.7 grains	3700 fps	24" barrel, 1:10" twist, 58-grain bullet
Lyman	40.5 grains	3490 fps	45.0 grains	3877 fps	24" barrel, 1:10" twist, 58-grain bullet
Lyman	38.0 grains	3488 fps	42.0 grains	3772 fps	24" barrel, 1:10" twist, 60-grain bullet
Sierra	39.7 grains	3300 fps	40.8 grains	3400 fps	22" barrel, 1:9$\frac{1}{8}$" twist, 60-grain bullet

*The Barnes manual does not list IMR 4895 powder for its 62-grain bullet. The Hornady manual lists Hodgdon's H4895 powder, which has a slightly different burning rate than IMR 4895 powder. The Nosler and Speer manuals do not list a 58-, 60-, or 62-grain bullet.

IMR 4895 Powder—65-Grain Bullet*

Manual	Minimum Charge	Muzzle Velocity	Maximum Charge	Muzzle Velocity	Barrel Length, Twist Rate
Hornady	32.5 grains	3100 fps	38.4 grains	3500 fps	24" barrel, 1:10"
Lyman	38.7 grains	3328 fps	43.0 grains	3645 fps	24" barrel, 1:10"

*The Barnes. Nosler, Sierra, and Speer manuals do not list a 65-grain bullet. The Hornady manual lists Hodgdon's H4895 powder, which has a slightly different burning rate than IMR 4895 powder.

IMR 4895 Powder—70-Grain Bullet*

Manual	Minimum Charge	Muzzle Velocity	Maximum Charge	Muzzle Velocity	Barrel Length, Twist Rate
Hornady	31.9 grains	3000 fps	37.8 grains	3400 fps	24" barrel, 1:10"
Lyman	36.0 grains	3257 fps	40.0 grains	3539 fps	24" barrel, 1:10"
Nosler	36.0 grains	3160 fps	40.0 grains	3483 fps	24" barrel, 1:10"
Sierra	36.0 grains	3000 fps	39.0 grains	3300 fps	22" barrel, 1:9$\frac{1}{8}$"
Speer	39.0 grains	3303 fps	43.0 grains	3540 fps	24" barrel

*The Barnes manual does not list a 70-grain bullet. The Hornady manual lists Hodgdon's H4895 powder, which has a slightly different burning rate than IMR 4895 powder.

IMR 4895 Powder—75-Grain Bullet*

Manual	Minimum Charge	Muzzle Velocity	Maximum Charge	Muzzle Velocity	Barrel Length, Twist Rate
Hornady	31.4 grains	2900 fps	36.9 grains	3300 fps	24" barrel, 1:10"
Lyman	34.0 grains	3041 fps	39.0 grains	3407 fps	24" barrel, 1:10"
Sierra	36.0 grains	3000 fps	39.0 grains	3300 fps	22" barrel, 1:9$\frac{1}{8}$"
Speer	38.5 grains	3183 fps	42.5 grains	3407 fps	24" barrel

*The Barnes and Nosler manuals do not list a 75-grain bullet. The Hornady manual lists Hodgdon's H4895 powder, which has a slightly different burning rate than IMR 4895 powder.

IMR 4895 Powder—80-Grain Bullet*

Manual	Minimum Charge	Muzzle Velocity	Maximum Charge	Muzzle Velocity	Barrel Length, Twist Rate
Hornady	31.9 grains	2900 fps	35.9 grains	3200 fps	26" barrel, 1:10"
Lyman	32.0 grains	2873 fps	38.5 grains	3308 fps	24" barrel, 1:10"
Nosler	35.0 grains	3045 fps	39.0 grains	3321 fps	24" barrel, 1:10"
Sierra	34.5 grains	2800 fps	37.8 grains	3100 fps	22" barrel, 1:9$\frac{1}{8}$"
Speer	38.0 grains	3049 fps	42.0 grains	3330 fps	24" barrel

*The Barnes manual does not list an 80-grain bullet. The Hornady manual lists Hodgdon's H4895 powder, which has a slightly different burning rate than IMR 4895 powder.

IMR 4350 Powder—55-Grain Bullet*

Manual	Minimum Charge	Muzzle Velocity	Maximum Charge	Muzzle Velocity	Barrel Length, Twist Rate
Sierra	44.9 grains	3300 fps	46.7 grains	3500 fps	22" barrel, 1:9$\frac{1}{8}$"

*Only the Sierra manual list loads for the 55-grain bullet using IMR 4350 powder.

IMR 4350 Powder—58/60/62-Grain Bullets*

Manual	Minimum Charge	Muzzle Velocity	Maximum Charge	Muzzle Velocity	Barrel Length, Twist Rate
Barnes	43.0 grains	3455 fps	47.0 grains	3699 fps	24" barrel, 1:10" twist, 62-grain bullet
Lyman	45.0 grains	3331 fps	50.0 grains	3776 fps	24" barrel, 1:10" twist, 58-grain bullet
Lyman	42.0 grains	3291 fps	47.0 grains	3726 fps	24" barrel, 1:10" twist, 60-grain bullet
Sierra	44.9 grains	3300 fps	46.7 grains	3500 fps	22" barrel, 1:9$\frac{1}{8}$" twist, 60-grain bullet

*The Hornady manual does not list IMR 4350 powder for its 58-grain bullet. The Nosler and Speer manuals do not list a 58-, 60-, or 62-grain bullet.

IMR 4350 Powder—65-Grain Bullet*

Manual	Minimum Charge	Muzzle Velocity	Maximum Charge	Muzzle Velocity	Barrel Length, Twist Rate
Lyman	43.2 grains	3209 fps	48.0 grains	3602 fps	24" barrel, 1:10"

*The Barnes, Nosler, Sierra, and Speer manuals do not list a 65-grain bullet. The Hornady manual does not list IMR 4350 powder for its 65-grain bullet.

IMR 4350 Powder—70-Grain Bullet*

Manual	Minimum Charge	Muzzle Velocity	Maximum Charge	Muzzle Velocity	Barrel Length, Twist Rate
Hornady	44.0 grains	3200 fps	47.9 grains	3500 fps	26" barrel, 1:10"
Lyman	40.0 grains	3193 fps	45.5 grains	3578 fps	24" barrel, 1:10"
Nosler	43.0 grains	3250 fps	47.0 grains	3610 fps	24" barrel, 1:10"
Sierra	41.6 grains	3000 fps	44.6 grains	3300 fps	22" barrel, 1:9$\frac{1}{8}$"
Speer	44.5 grains	3135 fps	48.5 grains	3461 fps	24" barrel

*The Barnes manual does not list a 70-grain bullet. The Hornady manual lists Hodgdon's H4350 powder, which has a slightly different burning rate than IMR 4350 powder.

IMR 4350 Powder—75-Grain Bullet*

Manual	Minimum Charge	Muzzle Velocity	Maximum Charge	Muzzle Velocity	Barrel Length, Twist Rate
Hornady	42.9 grains	3100 fps	46.7 grains	3400 fps	24" barrel, 1:10"
Lyman	40.0 grains	3160 fps	45.0 grains	3425 fps	24" barrel, 1:10"
Sierra	41.6 grains	3000 fps	44.6 grains	3300 fps	22" barrel, 1:9$\frac{1}{8}$"
Speer	44.0 grains	3043 fps	48.0 grains	3384 fps	24" barrel

*The Barnes and Nosler manuals do not list a 75-grain bullet. The Hornady manual lists Hodgdon's H4350 powder, which has a slightly different burning rate than IMR 4350 powder.

IMR 4350 Powder—80-Grain Bullet*

Manual	Minimum Charge	Muzzle Velocity	Maximum Charge	Muzzle Velocity	Barrel Length, Twist Rate
Hornady	40.6 grains	3000 fps	44.4 grains	3200 fps	24" barrel, 1:10"
Lyman	39.0 grains	3035 fps	41.5 grains	3194 fps	24" barrel, 1:10"
Nosler	41.0 grains	3168 fps	45.0 grains	3438 fps	24" barrel, 1:10"
Sierra	39.6 grains	2800 fps	42.2 grains	3000 fps	22" barrel, 1:9$\frac{1}{8}$"
Speer	43.0 grains	3023 fps	47.0 grains	3340 fps	24" barrel

*The Barnes manual does not list an 80-grain bullet. The Hornady manual lists Hodgdon's H4350 powder, which has a slightly different burning rate than IMR 4350 powder.

IMR 4064 Powder—55-Grain Bullet*

Manual	Minimum Charge	Muzzle Velocity	Maximum Charge	Muzzle Velocity	Barrel Length, Twist Rate
Nosler	41.5 grains	3549 fps	45.5 grains	3970 fps	24" barrel, 1:10"
Sierra	40.2 grains	3300 fps	42.9 grains	3600 fps	22" barrel, 1:9$\frac{1}{8}$"

*Only the Nosler and Sierra manuals list a 55-grain bullet. The Sierra manual lists Accurate AA4064, which has a slightly different burning rate than IMR 4064 powder.

IMR 4064 Powder—58/60/62-Grain Bullets*

Manual	Minimum Charge	Muzzle Velocity	Maximum Charge	Muzzle Velocity	Barrel Length, Twist Rate
Hornady	38.5 grains	3300 fps	43.6 grains	3800 fps	24" barrel, 1:10" twist, 58-grain bullet
Sierra	40.2 grains	3300 fps	42.9 grains	3600 fps	22" barrel, 1:9$\frac{1}{8}$" twist, 60-grain bullet

*The Barnes manual does not list IMR 4064 powder for its 62-grain bullet. The Lyman manual does not list IMR 4064 powder for the 58-grain bullet. The Nosler and Speer manuals do not list a 58-, 60-, or 62-grain bullet. The Sierra manual lists Accurate AA4064, which has a slightly different burning rate than IMR 4064 powder.

IMR 4064 Powder—65-Grain Bullet*

Manual	Minimum Charge	Muzzle Velocity	Maximum Charge	Muzzle Velocity	Barrel Length, Twist Rate
Hornady	35.4 grains	3100 fps	41.2 grains	3600 fps	24" barrel, 1:10"
Lyman	39.6 grains	3369 fps	44.0 grains	3696 fps	24" barrel, 1:10"

*The Barnes, Nosler, Sierra, and Speer manuals do not list a 65-grain bullet.

IMR 4064 Powder—70-Grain Bullet*

Manual	Minimum Charge	Muzzle Velocity	Maximum Charge	Muzzle Velocity	Barrel Length, Twist Rate
Hornady	33.5 grains	3000 fps	41.0 grains	3500 fps	24" barrel, 1:10"
Lyman	37.0 grains	3316 fps	41.0 grains	3610 fps	24" barrel, 1:10"
Nosler	37.5 grains	3168 fps	41.5 grains	3478 fps	24" barrel, 1:10"
Sierra	35.8 grains	3000 fps	39.4 grains	3300 fps	22" barrel, 1:9$\frac{1}{8}$"
Speer	39.0 grains	3089 fps	43.0 grains	3419 fps	24" barrel

*The Barnes manual does not list a 70-grain bullet. The Speer manual lists Accurate AA4064, which has a slightly different burning rate than IMR 4064 powder.

IMR 4064 Powder—75-Grain Bullet*

Manual	Minimum Charge	Muzzle Velocity	Maximum Charge	Muzzle Velocity	Barrel Length, Twist Rate
Hornady	33.0 grains	2900 fps	38.9 grains	3300 fps	24" barrel, 1:10"
Lyman	36.0 grains	3127 fps	40.5 grains	3460 fps	24" barrel, 1:10"
Sierra	35.8 grains	3000 fps	39.4 grains	3300 fps	22" barrel, 1:9$\frac{1}{8}$"
Speer	38.5 grains	2930 fps	42.5 grains	3301 fps	24" barrel

*The Barnes and Nosler manuals do not list IMR 4064 powder for the 75-grain bullet. The Speer manual lists Accurate AA4064, which is equivalent to IMR 4064 powder.

IMR 4064 Powder—80-Grain Bullet*

Manual	Minimum Charge	Muzzle Velocity	Maximum Charge	Muzzle Velocity	Barrel Length, Twist Rate
Hornady	33.0 grains	2900 fps	38.8 grains	3300 fps	24" barrel, 1:10"
Lyman	34.0 grains	2958 fps	39.5 grains	3378 fps	24" barrel, 1:10"
Nosler	36.0 grains	3124 fps	40.0 grains	3393 fps	24" barrel, 1:10"
Sierra	34.1 grains	2800 fps	38.0 grains	3100 fps	22" barrel, 1:9$\frac{1}{8}$"

*The Barnes manual does not list an 80-grain bullet. The Speer manual does not list IMR 4064 powder for its 80-grain bullet.

Hodgdon VARGET Powder—55-Grain Bullet*

Manual	Minimum Charge	Muzzle Velocity	Maximum Charge	Muzzle Velocity	Barrel Length, Twist Rate
Nosler	41.5 grains	3575 fps	45.5 grains	3941 fps	24" barrel, 1:10"
Sierra	39.7 grains	3300 fps	43.0 grains	3600 fps	22" barrel, 1:9$\frac{1}{8}$"

*Only the Nosler and Sierra manuals list a 55-grain bullet.

Hodgdon VARGET Powder—58/60/62-Grain Bullets*

Manual	Minimum Charge	Muzzle Velocity	Maximum Charge	Muzzle Velocity	Barrel Length, Twist Rate
Hornady	37.5 grains	3300 fps	44.2 grains	3800 fps	24" barrel, 1:10" twist, 58-grain bullet
Lyman	40.9 grains	3526 fps	45.5 grains	3891 fps	24" barrel, 1:10" twist, 58-grain bullet
Sierra	39.7 grains	3300 fps	43.0 grains	3600 fps	22" barrel, 1:9$\frac{1}{8}$" twist, 60-grain bullet

*The Barnes manual does not list Varget powder for its 62-grain bullet. The Lyman manual does not list Varget powder for the 60-grain bullet. The Nosler and Speer manuals do not list a 58-, 60-, or 62-grain bullet.

Hodgdon VARGET Powder—65-Grain Bullet*

Manual	Minimum Charge	Muzzle Velocity	Maximum Charge	Muzzle Velocity	Barrel Length, Twist Rate
Hornady	35.1 grains	3100 fps	41.7 grains	3600 fps	24" barrel, 1:10"
Lyman	38.2 grains	3342 fps	42.0 grains	3644 fps	24" barrel, 1:10"

*The Barnes, Nosler, Sierra, and Speer manuals do not list a 65-grain bullet.

Hodgdon VARGET Powder—70-Grain Bullet*

Manual	Minimum Charge	Muzzle Velocity	Maximum Charge	Muzzle Velocity	Barrel Length, Twist Rate
Lyman	37.5 grains	3301 fps	41.7 grains	3553 fps	24" barrel, 1:10"
Nosler	38.0 grains	3338 fps	42.0 grains	3616 fps	24" barrel, 1:10"
Sierra	36.7 grains	3000 fps	41.1 grains	3400 fps	22" barrel, 1:9$\frac{1}{8}$"
Speer	39.0 grains	3236 fps	43.0 grains	3515 fps	24" barrel

*The Barnes manual does not list a 70-grain bullet. The Hornady manual does not list Varget powder for its 70-grain bullet.

Hodgdon VARGET Powder—75-Grain Bullet*

Manual	Minimum Charge	Muzzle Velocity	Maximum Charge	Muzzle Velocity	Barrel Length, Twist Rate
Lyman	37.5 grains	3181 fps	41.0 grains	3446 fps	24" barrel, 1:10"
Sierra	36.7 grains	3000 fps	41.1 grains	3400 fps	22" barrel, 1:9$\frac{1}{8}$"
Speer	38.0 grains	3186 fps	42.0 grains	3388 fps	24" barrel

*The Barnes and Nosler manuals do not list a 45-grain bullet. The Hornady manual does not list Varget powder for the 75-grain bullet.

Hodgdon VARGET Powder—80-Grain Bullet*

Manual	Minimum Charge	Muzzle Velocity	Maximum Charge	Muzzle Velocity	Barrel Length, Twist Rate
Nosler	36.0 grains	3112 fps	40.0 grains	3371 fps	24" barrel, 1:10"
Sierra	34.7 grains	2800 fps	38.0 grains	3100 fps	22" barrel, 1:9$\frac{1}{8}$"
Speer	38.0 grains	3094 fps	42.0 grains	3321 fps	24" barrel

*The Barnes manual does not list an 80-grain bullet. The Hornady and Lyman manuals do not list Varget powder for the 80-grain bullet.

RANGE TESTS

The day I tested the .243 Winchester featured a mostly sunny sky with a moderate wind from 6 o'clock and a temperature in the mid-70s. For the factory ammo test, I chose the Winchester 80-grain pointed soft point ammunition, the results of which can be seen on the next page.

Group 1 measured 2.9" center to center; group 2 measured 2.6" center to center. This isn't good accuracy for varmint shooting. Also, the light barrel, even though I free floated it, appears to have quite a whip—each different load and bullet weight shot to a markedly different point of impact.

The Oehler chronograph measured an average velocity of 3219 fps for the Winchester 80-grain factory ammo. This is about 100 fps lower than the 3350 fps listed by Winchester for its 80-grain bullet.

.243 Winchester—Factory Ammo Group 1.

.243 Winchester—Factory Ammo Group 2.

```
2877-01-2875-
2863-02-2861-
2930-03-2926-
2871-04-2869-
2888-05-2886-
2960-06-2908-
- - - - - - -
06-2926-+
06-2861- -
06-0065-T
06-2887-M
06-0024-$
- - - - - - -
```

The Oehler chronograph data for the Winchester 80-grain factory ammunition indicates an average velocity (M) of 3219 fps and a standard deviation ($) of 26 fps.

This low standard deviation reading indicates consistent ammo.

Following are the test results for my .243 Winchester handload, which consisted of the Sierra 75-grain hollow point bullet, 39 grains of Hornady's Varget powder, and the CCI 200 primer.

The first group measured 1.8" and the second group measured 1.46" with four shots in 0.92"—the leftmost shot is a double. This is reasonable accuracy for a rifle that will be used for both varmints and medium-sized game.

The Oehler chronograph measured an average velocity of 3056 fps for my handload. This is about 150 fps lower than the data provided by Sierra.

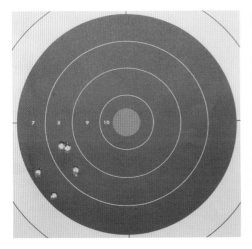

.243 Winchester—Handload Group 1.

.243 Winchester—Handload Group 2.

The Oehler chronograph measured an average muzzle velocity (M) of 3056 fps for the .243 Winchester handload. The standard deviation ($) of 23 indicates good consistency.
* The average velocity is about 150 fps lower than that listed in the Sierra manual.*

```
3581-01-3568-
3490-02-3478-
3502-03-3491-
3571-04-3558-
3565-05-3557-
3587-06-3568-
3623-07-3601-
3616-08-3598-
3590-09-3573-
3623-10-3603-
- - - - - - - -
        10-3603-+
        10-3478--
        10-0125-T
        10-3559-M
        10-0043-$
- - - - - - - -
```

105

TRAJECTORY TABLES

The following trajectory tables were developed using the Handloads.com ballistic calculator. The tables are based on the line of sight (LOS) being 1.5 inches above the line of fire (LOF). All tabular data is expressed in inches.

55-Grain Bullet (BC = .225)

Muzzle Velocity (fps)	Muzzle	100 yards	200 yards	300 yards	400 yards
	−1.5	0.0	−1.4	−6.7	−17.3
4000	−1.5	0.7	0.0	−4.6	−14.5
	−1.5	2.2	3.1	0.0	−8.3
	−1.5	0.0	−1.6	−7.3	−18.5
3900	−1.5	0.8	0.0	−4.9	−15.3
	−1.5	2.4	3.3	0.0	−8.8
	−1.5	0.0	−1.7	−7.8	−20.0
3800	−1.5	0.9	0.0	−5.2	−16.3
	−1.5	2.6	3.5	0.0	−9.4
	−1.5	0.0	−1.9	−8.5	−21.2
3700	−1.5	1.0	0.0	−5.6	−17.4
	−1.5	2.8	3.7	0.0	−10.0
	−1.5	0.0	−2.1	−9.1	−22.8
3600	−1.5	1.1	0.0	−5.9	−18.5
	−1.5	3.0	4.0	0.0	−10.6
	−1.5	0.0	−2.3	−9.9	−24.5
3500	−1.5	1.2	0.0	−6.4	−19.8
	−1.5	3.3	4.2	0.0	−11.4
	−1.5	0.0	−2.6	−10.7	−26.0
3400	−1.5	1.3	0.0	−6.8	−21.2
	−1.5	3.6	4.6	0.0	−12.2
	−1.5	0.0	−2.8	−11.6	−28.5
3300	−1.5	1.4	0.0	−7.3	−22.8
	−1.5	3.9	4.9	0.0	−13.0

60-Grain Bullet (BC = .250)

Muzzle Velocity (fps)	Muzzle	100 yards	200 yards	300 yards	400 yards
	−1.5	0.0	−1.5	−6.8	−17.2
3900	−1.5	0.7	0.0	−4.6	−14.3
	−1.5	2.3	3.1	0.0	−8.1
	−1.5	0.0	−1.7	−7.4	−18.4
3800	−1.5	0.8	0.0	−4.9	−15.2
	−1.5	2.5	3.3	0.0	−8.6
	−1.5	0.0	−1.8	−8.0	−19.8
3700	−1.5	0.9	0.0	−5.2	−16.1
	−1.5	2.7	3.5	0.0	−9.2
	−1.5	0.0	−2.0	−8.6	−21.2
3600	−1.5	1.0	0.0	−5.6	−17.2
	−1.5	2.9	3.7	0.0	−9.8
	−1.5	0.0	−2.2	−9.3	−22.8
3500	−1.5	1.1	0.0	−6.0	−18.4
	−1.5	3.1	4.0	0.0	−10.4
	−1.5	0.0	−2.5	−10.1	−24.6
3400	−1.5	1.2	0.0	−6.4	−19.7
	−1.5	3.4	4.3	0.0	−11.1
	−1.5	0.0	−2.7	−10.9	−26.5
3300	−1.5	1.4	0.0	−6.9	−21.1
	−1.5	3.7	4.6	0.0	−12.0
	−1.5	0.0	−3.0	−11.9	−28.7
3200	−1.5	1.5	0.0	−7.4	−22.7
	−1.5	4.0	4.9	0.0	−12.8

65-Grain Bullet (BC = .280)

Muzzle Velocity (fps)	Muzzle	100 yards	200 yards	300 yards	400 yards
	−1.5	0.0	−1.7	−7.5	−18.5
3700	−1.5	0.9	0.0	−4.9	−15.0
	−1.5	2.5	3.3	0.0	−8.5
	−1.5	0.0	−1.9	−8.1	−19.9
3600	−1.5	1.0	0.0	−5.3	−16.0
	−1.5	2.7	3.5	0.0	−9.0
	−1.5	0.0	−2.1	−8.8	−21.4
3500	−1.5	1.1	0.0	−5.6	−17.1
	−1.5	2.9	3.8	0.0	−9.6
	−1.5	0.0	−2.3	−9.5	−23.0
3400	−1.5	1.2	0.0	−6.0	−18.3
	−1.5	3.2	4.0	0.0	−10.3
	−1.5	0.0	−2.6	−10.4	−24.8
3300	−1.5	1.3	0.0	−6.5	−19.7
	−1.5	3.5	4.3	0.0	−11.0
	−1.5	0.0	−2.9	−11.3	−26.8
3200	−1.5	1.4	0.0	−7.0	−21.1
	−1.5	3.8	4.7	0.0	−11.8
	−1.5	0.0	−3.1	−12.2	−29.0
3100	−1.5	1.6	0.0	−7.5	−22.7
	−1.5	4.1	5.0	0.0	−12.7

70-Grain Bullet (BC = .270)

Muzzle Velocity (fps)	Muzzle	100 yards	200 yards	300 yards	400 yards
	−1.5	0.0	−1.9	−8.3	−20.3
3600	−1.5	1.0	0.0	−5.4	−16.4
	−1.5	2.8	3.6	0.0	−9.2
	−1.5	0.0	−2.1	−9.0	−21.8
3500	−1.5	1.1	0.0	−5.7	−17.5
	−1.5	3.0	3.8	0.0	−9.9
	−1.5	0.0	−2.4	−9.7	−23.5
3400	−1.5	1.2	0.0	−6.2	−18.7
	−1.5	3.2	4.1	0.0	−10.5
	−1.5	0.0	−2.6	−10.5	−25.3
3300	−1.5	1.3	0.0	−6.6	−20.1
	−1.5	3.5	4.4	0.0	−11.3
	−1.5	0.0	−2.9	−11.4	−27.4
3200	−1.5	1.4	0.0	−7.1	−21.6
	−1.5	3.8	4.7	0.0	−12.1
	−1.5	0.0	−3.2	−12.4	−29.7
3100	−1.5	1.6	0.0	−7.7	−23.3
	−1.5	4.1	5.1	0.0	−13.1
	−1.5	0.0	−3.5	−13.6	−32.2
3000	−1.5	1.8	0.0	−8.3	−25.1
	−1.5	4.5	5.5	0.0	−14.1

75-Grain Bullet (BC = .300)

Muzzle Velocity (fps)	Muzzle	100 yards	200 yards	300 yards	400 yards
	−1.5	0.0	−2.3	−9.3	−22.2
3400	−1.5	1.1	0.0	−5.9	−17.6
	−1.5	3.1	3.9	0.0	−9.8
	−1.5	0.0	−2.5	−10.1	−23.9
3300	−1.5	1.3	0.0	−6.3	−18.9
	−1.5	3.4	4.2	0.0	−10.5
	−1.5	0.0	−2.8	−10.9	−28.9
3200	−1.5	1.4	0.0	−6.8	−20.3
	−1.5	3.6	4.5	0.0	−11.3
	−1.5	0.0	−3.1	−11.9	−28.0
3100	−1.5	1.5	0.0	−7.3	−21.9
	−1.5	4.0	4.9	0.0	−12.1
	−1.5	0.0	−3.4	−12.9	−30.4
3000	−1.5	1.7	0.0	−7.9	−23.6
	−1.5	4.3	5.2	0.0	−13.1
	−1.5	0.0	−3.7	−14.1	−33.0
2900	−1.5	1.9	0.0	−8.5	−25.5
	−1.5	4.7	5.7	0.0	−14.2

80-Grain Bullet (BC = .320)

Muzzle Velocity (fps)	Muzzle	100 yards	200 yards	300 yards	400 yards
	−1.5	0.0	−2.2	−9.0	−21.5
3400	−1.5	1.1	0.0	−5.7	−17.0
	−1.5	3.0	3.8	0.0	−9.5
	−1.5	0.0	−2.5	−9.8	−23.2
3300	−1.5	1.2	0.0	−6.1	−18.3
	−1.5	3.3	4.1	0.0	−10.1
	−1.5	0.0	−2.7	−10.6	−25.0
3200	−1.5	1.4	0.0	−6.6	−19.6
	−1.5	3.6	4.4	0.0	−10.9
	−1.5	0.0	−3.0	−11.6	−27.1
3100	−1.5	1.5	0.0	−7.1	−21.1
	−1.5	3.9	4.7	0.0	−11.7
	−1.5	0.0	−3.3	−12.6	−29.4
3000	−1.5	1.7	0.0	−7.6	−22.8
	−1.5	4.2	5.1	0.0	−12.6
	−1.5	0.0	−3.7	−13.8	−31.9
2900	−1.5	1.8	0.0	−8.3	−24.6
	−1.5	4.6	5.5	0.0	−13.6
	−1.5	0.0	−4.1	−15.1	−34.8
2800	−1.5	2.0	0.0	−9.0	−26.7
	−1.5	5.0	6.0	0.0	−14.7

Chapter 8

6mm Remington

In 1955, both Remington and Winchester debuted new 6mm cartridges. Winchester released the .243 Winchester cartridge in the Model 70 as a dual purpose varmint and medium game round. Barrels chambered for the .243 Winchester had a 1-10" twist, which was suitable for bullet weights from 70 grain (varmints) to 105 grain (medium game). Remington, however, envisioned the .244 Remington cartridge (which was basically the .257 Roberts necked down to 6mm with about a 5° sharper shoulder angle) more as a varmint round and gave their barrels a twist of 1-12" to favor the lighter varmint bullets. The heaviest bullet they offered in factory ammunition for their .244 Remington was 90 grains. The 1-12" twist would not always stabilize the heavier 100 grain bullet.

Some of the credit for the early development of the .244 Remington goes to Fred Huntington, the founder of RCBS, who developed the .243 Rock Chucker wildcat cartridge and to Warren Page, the gun editor of *Field & Stream* magazine, who created the .240 Page Pooper.

The .243 Winchester quickly became popular with hunters as a varmint/medium game cartridge. The .244 Remington, mostly because of the slower twist, did not. Another factor affecting the popularity of the .244 Remington was that Remington's center fire bolt action rifles (the Model 721 and Model 722), while quite accurate and well designed, were somewhat spartan in appearance – especially when compared to the Winchester Model 70, the "Rifleman's Rifle."

In 1962, Remington transformed their plain Jane Model 721/722 into a much more pleasing Model 700. The new rifle became a worthy competitor to Winchester's Model 70. A year later, Remington reintroduced the .244 Remington as the 6mm Remington. (Remington had earlier, in 1958, changed the rifling twist for this cartridge to a faster 1-9" twist) The 6mm Remington (a.k.a. the .244 Remington) was now marketed as a dual purpose varmint and medium game cartridge like its competitor, the .243 Winchester. Unfortunately, the .243 Winchester had a great head start and the 6mm Remington never caught up. The 6mm Remington is a classic example of a great cartridge that is no longer popular. Today, no rifles are offered in this chambering by any of the large firearms manufacturers. This is unfortunate, though, because the 6mm Remington case is slightly larger than that of the .243 Winchester and, on average, delivers about 100 fps more velocity.

THE RUGER NO. 1 VARMINTER

Bill Ruger was somewhat of a gambler when it came to designing new rifles, but he had a good winning streak, as evidenced by the No.

Author's Ruger Model No. 1 Varminter—6mm Remington.

1 single-shot rifle. The Ruger No. 1 is a modern version of the British Farquharson falling block rifle—a classic single-shot rifle from the 19th century.

The No. 1 has classic lines just like its ancestor, but is truly a modern version in every respect. My model, the Varminter, is designed specifically for varmint hunting. It has a heavy 24 inch barrel, target blocks for scope mounting, and a wide fore-end. The rifling twist for the 6mm Remington is 1:9".

The trigger is slightly adjustable, and I was able to set it to three and a half pounds. There is no creep. The trigger breaks cleanly.

The scope is a variable power Leupold VX-2 4-12×40mm AO with the LR Duplex reticle and $\frac{1}{4}$ MOA windage and elevation adjustments. The scope is mounted using the Ruger rings that were included with the rifle.

With its 24 inch medium-heavy barrel and wide forearm, the No. 1 Varminter, in combination with its scope and mounts, weighs slightly less than ten pounds.

Because this book is about varmint rifles and cartridges, I am restricting the following information about 6mm Remington factory ammo and handloads to bullet weights of no heavier than 80 grains.

6MM REMINGTON FACTORY AMMO

Factory ammunition for the 6mm Remington cartridge that is suitable for varmint hunting is limited to the 80-grain soft point from Federal. Ironically, Remington, the originator of the 6mm Remington, no longer offers any factory ammunition for this cartridge.

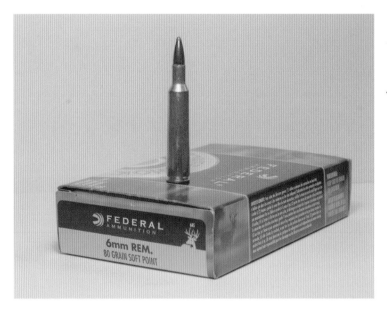

The 6mm Remington, while not as popular as the .243 Winchester, is a fine dual-purpose cartridge for both varmints and medium-size game, such as deer and antelope.

Federal Premium Ammunition

Bullet Weight (Grains)	Bullet Type	Velocity (fps)					Energy (ft-lbs)				
		Muzzle	100 yards	200 yards	300 yards	400 yards	Muzzle	100 yards	200 yards	300 yards	400 yards
80	Soft point	3400	3117	2851	2601	2364	2053	1725	1444	1202	993

HANDLOADING THE 6MM REMINGTON

When using the 6mm Remington for varmint hunting, handloading should definitely be considered. Handloaders will have more bullet selection when it comes to this cartridge. With the exception of Norma, all the other current reloading manuals list data for the 6mm Remington cartridge.

Barnes Reloading Manual Number 4

The Barnes manual lists loads for its 62-, 75-, and 85-grain bullets. For each bullet weight, Barnes identifies the powder that produces the most accurate loads. Vihtavuori N550 produced the most accurate loads for the 62-grain VG bullet, while Ramshot's Hunter powder was the most accurate load for the Barnes 75-grain BND Spitzer bullet.

Hornady Handbook of Cartridge Reloading, 8th Edition

Hornady includes loads for its 58-, 65-, 70-, 75-, 80-, 85/87-, 95/100-, and 105-grain bullets. IMR 4064 and Vihtavuori N160 powders produced the best groups during Hornady's testing of the 6mm Remington. For the purpose of developing varmint loads, we will only consider the loads for bullet weights from 58 to 80 grains.

Lyman Reloading Handbook, 49th Edition

The Lyman manual lists 6mm Remington loads for bullet weights from 60 to 100 grains. For developing varmint loads, we will consider the load data for the 60-, 70-, 75-, and 80-grain bullets. Lyman recommends IMR 4350 as the ideal powder for the 6mm Remington.

Nosler Reloading Guide No. 6

Nosler lists loads for its 55-, 70-, 80-, 85-, 90-, 95-, and 100-grain 6mm bullets. The most accurate powder for the Nosler 55-grain bullet was Winchester's W760 powder. For the Nosler 70-grain bullet, Vihtavuori N160 powder proved the most accurate. For the 80-grain bullets, the most accurate powder tested was IMR 4064.

Sierra 5th Edition Reloading Manual

Sierra includes load tables for its 55-, 60-, 70-, 75-, 80-, 85-, 90-, 100-, and 107-grain bullets. We will only consider the loads for the 55- to 80-grain bullets, as they are applicable to varmint shooting.

Sierra's accuracy load for its 55- and 60-grain bullets was with 43.5 grains of Hodgdon's Varget powder; for hunting, 43.7 grains of Accurate's AA4064. The best accuracy for the Sierra 70- and 75-grain bullets was obtained using Vihtavuori N140 powder. The accuracy load for the 80-grain bullet was 38.3 grains of IMR 4895 powder. The best hunting load for this bullet weight was 41.2 grains of Vihtavuori N140 powder.

Speer Reloading Manual #14

The Speer manual includes 6mm Remington loads for its 70-, 75-, 80-, 85-, 90-, 100-, and 105-grain bullets. Speer lists many of the powders that most of the other manuals do, but does not identify any powders as producing the best accuracy. Also, the Speer manual does not list the twist rate for the 6mm Remington test firearm barrel.

The following tables list some loads from the current reloading manuals for each bullet weight from 55 to 80 grains. I consider these weights suitable for varmint shooting with the 6mm Remington.

IMR 4895 Powder—55-Grain Bullet*

Manual	Minimum Charge	Muzzle Velocity	Maximum Charge	Muzzle Velocity	Barrel Length, Twist Rate
Sierra	39.6 grains	3200 fps	41.9 grains	3400 fps	22" barrel, 1:9"

*Only the Nosler and Sierra manuals list loads for the 55-grain bullet. The Nosler manual does not list IMR 4895 powder for the 55-grain bullet.

IMR 4895 Powder—58/60/62-Grain Bullets*

Manual	Minimum Charge	Muzzle Velocity	Maximum Charge	Muzzle Velocity	Barrel Length, Twist Rate
Hornady	37.4 grains	3300 fps	43.7 grains	3800 fps	22" barrel, 1:9" twist, 58-grain bullet
Lyman	38.0 grains	3279 fps	42.5 grains	3623 fps	24" barrel, 1:9" twist, 60-grain bullet
Sierra	39.6 grains	3200 fps	41.9 grains	3400 fps	22" barrel, 1:9" twist, 60-grain bullet

*The Barnes manual does not list IMR 4895 powder for its 62-grain bullet. The Hornady manual lists Hodgdon's H4895 powder, which has a slightly different burning rate than IMR 4895 powder. The Nosler and Speer manuals do not list a 58-, 60-, or 62-grain bullet.

IMR 4895 Powder—65-Grain Bullet*

Manual	Minimum Charge	Muzzle Velocity	Maximum Charge	Muzzle Velocity	Barrel Length, Twist Rate
Hornady	34.4 grains	3100 fps	41.8 grains	3600 fps	22" barrel, 1:9"

*Only the Hornady manual lists a 65-grain bullet. The Hornady manual lists Hodgdon's H4895 powder, which has a slightly different burning rate than IMR 4895 powder.

IMR 4895 Powder—70-Grain Bullet*

Manual	Minimum Charge	Muzzle Velocity	Maximum Charge	Muzzle Velocity	Barrel Length, Twist Rate
Hornady	31.9 grains	2900 fps	41.0 grains	3400 fps	22" barrel, 1:9"
Lyman	37.0 grains	3067 fps	42.0 grains	3448 fps	24" barrel, 1:9"
Nosler	36.0 grains	3218 fps	40.0 grains	3511 fps	24" barrel, 1:10"
Sierra	38.0 grains	3000 fps	40.5 grains	3200 fps	22" barrel, 1:9"
Speer	38.0 grains	3111 fps	42.0 grains	3381 fps	24" barrel

*The Barnes manual does not list a 70-grain bullet. The Hornady manual lists Hodgdon's H4895 powder, which has a slightly different burning rate than IMR 4895 powder.

IMR 4895 Powder—75-Grain Bullet*

Manual	Minimum Charge	Muzzle Velocity	Maximum Charge	Muzzle Velocity	Barrel Length, Twist Rate
Hornady	33.6 grains	2900 fps	40.5 grains	3400 fps	22" barrel, 1:9"
Lyman	37.0 grains	3105 fps	39.0 grains	3385 fps	24" barrel, 1:9"
Sierra	38.0 grains	3000 fps	40.5 grains	3200 fps	22" barrel, 1:9"
Speer	37.0 grains	2969 fps	41.0 grains	3248 fps	24" barrel

*The Barnes manual does not list IMR 4895 powder for the 75-grain bullet. The Hornady manual lists Hodgdon's H4895 powder, which has a slightly different burning rate than IMR 4895 powder. The Nosler Manual does not list a 75-grain bullet.

IMR 4895 Powder—80-Grain Bullet*

Manual	Minimum Charge	Muzzle Velocity	Maximum Charge	Muzzle Velocity	Barrel Length, Twist Rate
Hornady	32.3 grains	2800 fps	38.2 grains	3200 fps	22" barrel, 1:9"
Lyman	35.8 grains	3107 fps	40.0 grains	3325 fps	24" barrel, 1:9"
Nosler	35.5 grains	3107 fps	39.5 grains	3322 fps	24" barrel, 1:10"
Sierra	35.7 grains	2800 fps	39.6 grains	3100 fps	22" barrel, 1:9"
Speer	36.0 grains	2870 fps	40.0 grains	3139 fps	24" barrel

*The Barnes manual does not list an 80-grain bullet. The Hornady manual lists Hodgdon's H4895 powder, which has a slightly different burning rate than IMR 4895 powder.

IMR 4350 Powder—55-Grain Bullet*

Manual	Minimum Charge	Muzzle Velocity	Maximum Charge	Muzzle Velocity	Barrel Length, Twist Rate
Nosler	48.0 grains	3464 fps	52.0 grains	3808 fps	24" barrel, 1:10"
Sierra	45.9 grains	3200 fps	48.2 grains	3400 fps	22" barrel, 1:9"

*Only the Nosler and Sierra manuals list loads for the 55-grain bullet.

IMR 4350 Powder—58/60/62-Grain Bullets*

Manual	Minimum Charge	Muzzle Velocity	Maximum Charge	Muzzle Velocity	Barrel Length, Twist Rate
Barnes	45.0 grains	3394 fps	50.0 grains	3755 fps	24" barrel, 1:9" twist, 62-grain bullet
Lyman	42.0 grains	3021 fps	49.0 grains	3623 fps	24" barrel, 1:9" twist, 60-grain bullet
Sierra	45.9 grains	3200 fps	48.2 grains	3400 fps	22" barrel, 1:9" twist, 60-grain bullet

*The Hornady manual does not list IMR 4350 powder for its 58-grain bullet. The Nosler and Speer manuals do not list a 58-, 60-, or 62-grain bullet.

IMR 4350 Powder—65-Grain Bullet*

Manual	Minimum Charge	Muzzle Velocity	Maximum Charge	Muzzle Velocity	Barrel Length, Twist Rate
Hornady	44.4 grains	3100 fps	48.5 grains	3500 fps	22" barrel, 1:9"

*Only the Hornady manuals lists a 65-grain bullet. The Hornady manual lists A 4350 powder, which is equivalent to IMR 4350 powder.

IMR 4350 Powder—70-Grain Bullet*

Manual	Minimum Charge	Muzzle Velocity	Maximum Charge	Muzzle Velocity	Barrel Length, Twist Rate
Hornady	42.2 grains	2900 fps	47.1 grains	3300 fps	22" barrel, 1:9"
Lyman	42.0 grains	2976 fps	48.5 grains	3484 fps	24" barrel, 1:9"
Nosler	44.0 grains	3312 fps	48.0 grains	3596 fps	24" barrel, 1:10"
Sierra	43.8 grains	3000 fps	47.3 grains	3300 fps	22" barrel, 1:9"
Speer	45.0 grains	3040 fps	49.0 grains	3416 fps	24" barrel

*The Barnes manual does not list a 70-grain bullet. The Hornady manual lists A 4350 powder, which is equivalent to IMR 4350 powder.

IMR 4350 Powder—75-Grain Bullet*

Manual	Minimum Charge	Muzzle Velocity	Maximum Charge	Muzzle Velocity	Barrel Length, Twist Rate
Barnes	45.0 grains	3271 fps	48.5 grains	3548 fps	24" barrel, 1:9"
Hornady	42.0 grains	2900 fps	46.8 grains	3300 fps	22" barrel, 1:9"
Lyman	41.5 grains	2976 fps	48.0 grains	3448 fps	24" barrel, 1:9"
Sierra	43.8 grains	3000 fps	47.3 grains	3300 fps	22" barrel, 1:9"
Speer	44.0 grains	3064 fps	48.0 grains	3367 fps	24" barrel

*The Nosler manual does not list a 75-grain bullet. The Hornady manual lists A 4350 powder, which is equivalent to IMR 4350.

IMR 4350 Powder—80-Grain Bullet*

Manual	Minimum Charge	Muzzle Velocity	Maximum Charge	Muzzle Velocity	Barrel Length, Twist Rate
Hornady	41.6 grains	2800 fps	46.1 grains	3200 fps	22" barrel, 1:9"
Lyman	41.0 grains	2873 fps	47.0 grains	3367 fps	24" barrel, 1:9"
Nosler	43.0 grains	3111 fps	47.0 grains	3472 fps	24" barrel, 1:10"
Sierra	41.8 grains	2800 fps	46.5 grains	3200 fps	22" barrel, 1:9"
Speer	43.0 grains	2939 fps	47.0 grains	3266 fps	24" barrel

*The Barnes manual does not list an 80-grain bullet. The Hornady manual lists A 4350 powder, which is equivalent to IMR 4350 powder.

IMR 4064 Powder—55-Grain Bullet*

Manual	Minimum Charge	Muzzle Velocity	Maximum Charge	Muzzle Velocity	Barrel Length, Twist Rate
Sierra	40.2 grains	3200 fps	43.1 grains	3500 fps	24" barrel, 1:9"

*Only the Nosler and Sierra manuals list a 55-grain bullet. Only the Sierra manual lists IMR 4064 powder for the 55-grain bullet.

IMR 4064 Powder—58/60/62-Grain Bullets*

Manual	Minimum Charge	Muzzle Velocity	Maximum Charge	Muzzle Velocity	Barrel Length, Twist Rate
Hornady	40.1 grains	3300 fps	44.6 grains	3700 fps	22" barrel, 1:9" twist, 58-grain bullet
Lyman	38.0 grains	3164 fps	44.0 grains	3759 fps	24" barrel, 1:9" twist, 60-grain bullet
Sierra	40.2 grains	3200 fps	43.1 grains	3500 fps	22" barrel, 1:9" twist, 60-grain bullet

*The Barnes manual does not list IMR 4064 powder for its 62-grain bullet. The Nosler and Speer manuals do not list a 58-, 60-, or 62-grain bullet.

IMR 4064 Powder—65-Grain Bullet*

Manual	Minimum Charge	Muzzle Velocity	Maximum Charge	Muzzle Velocity	Barrel Length, Twist Rate
Hornady	37.3 grains	3100 fps	43.2 grains	3600 fps	22" barrel, 1:9"

*Only the Hornady manual lists a 65-grain bullet.

IMR 4064 Powder—70-Grain Bullet*

Manual	Minimum Charge	Muzzle Velocity	Maximum Charge	Muzzle Velocity	Barrel Length, Twist Rate
Hornady	34.1 grains	2900 fps	41.8 grains	3400 fps	22" barrel, 1:9"
Lyman	37.5 grains	3067 fps	43.5 grains	3584 fps	24" barrel, 1:9"
Sierra	38.5 grains	3000 fps	41.9 grains	3300 fps	22" barrel, 1:9"
Speer	40.0 grains	3119 fps	44.0 grains	3427 fps	24" barrel

*The Barnes manual does not list a 70-grain bullet. The Nosler manual does not list IMR 4064 powder for its 70-grain bullet.

IMR 4064 Powder—75-Grain Bullet*

Manual	Minimum Charge	Muzzle Velocity	Maximum Charge	Muzzle Velocity	Barrel Length, Twist Rate
Hornady	35.2 grains	2900 fps	42.5 grains	3400 fps	22" barrel, 1:9"
Lyman	37.0 grains	3048 fps	42.5 grains	3448 fps	24" barrel, 1:9"
Sierra	38.5 grains	3000 fps	41.9 grains	3300 fps	22" barrel, 1:9"
Speer	38.5 grains	3010 fps	42.5 grains	3272 fps	24" barrel

*The Barnes manual does not list IMR 4064 powder for the 75-grain bullet. The Nosler manual does not list a 75-grain bullet. The Speer manual lists Accurate AA4064, which is equivalent to IMR 4064 powder.

IMR 4064 Powder—80-Grain Bullet*

Manual	Minimum Charge	Muzzle Velocity	Maximum Charge	Muzzle Velocity	Barrel Length, Twist Rate
Hornady	34.3 grains	2800 fps	41.6 grains	3300 fps	22" barrel, 1:9"
Lyman	36.5 grains	2915 fps	42.0 grains	3390 fps	24" barrel, 1:9"
Nosler	38.0 grains	3179 fps	42.0 grains	3451 fps	24" barrel, 1:10"
Sierra	36.5 grains	2800 fps	40.2 grains	3100 fps	22" barrel, 1:9"
Speer	37.0 grains	2873 fps	41.0 grains	3123 fps	24" barrel

*The Barnes manual does not list an 80-grain bullet.

Hodgdon VARGET Powder—55-Grain Bullet*

Manual	Minimum Charge	Muzzle Velocity	Maximum Charge	Muzzle Velocity	Barrel Length, Twist Rate
Nosler	43.0 grains	3661 fps	47.0 grains	4002 fps	24" barrel, 1:10"
Sierra	41.1 grains	3200 fps	43.5 grains	3500 fps	22" barrel, 1:9"

*Only the Nosler and Sierra manuals list a 55-grain bullet.

Hodgdon VARGET Powder—58/60/62-Grain Bullets*

Manual	Minimum Charge	Muzzle Velocity	Maximum Charge	Muzzle Velocity	Barrel Length, Twist Rate
Hornady	39.2 grains	3300 fps	45.8 grains	3800 fps	22" barrel, 1:9" twist, 58-grain bullet
Lyman	39.0 grains	3456 fps	43.5 grains	3700 fps	24" barrel, 1:9" twist, 60-grain bullet
Sierra	41.1 grains	3200 fps	43.5 grains	3500 fps	22" barrel, 1:9" twist, 60-grain bullet

*The Barnes manual does not list Varget powder for its 62-grain bullet. The Nosler and Speer manuals do not list a 58-, 60-, or 62-grain bullet.

117

Hodgdon VARGET Powder—65-Grain Bullet*

Manual	Minimum Charge	Muzzle Velocity	Maximum Charge	Muzzle Velocity	Barrel Length, Twist Rate
Hornady	36.4 grains	3100 fps	42.5 grains	3500 fps	22" barrel, 1:9"

*Only the Hornady manual lists a 65-grain bullet.

Hodgdon VARGET Powder—70-Grain Bullet*

Manual	Minimum Charge	Muzzle Velocity	Maximum Charge	Muzzle Velocity	Barrel Length, Twist Rate
Hornady	33.9 grains	2900 fps	41.6 grains	3400 fps	22" barrel, 1:9"
Lyman	36.7 grains	3261 fps	41.0 grains	3555 fps	24" barrel, 1:9"
Sierra	38.8 grains	3000 fps	40.3 grains	3100 fps	22" barrel, 1:9"

*The Barnes manual does not list a 70-grain bullet. The Nosler and Speer manuals do not list Varget powder for the 70-grain bullet.

Hodgdon VARGET Powder—75-Grain Bullet*

Manual	Minimum Charge	Muzzle Velocity	Maximum Charge	Muzzle Velocity	Barrel Length, Twist Rate
Hornady	34.5 grains	2900 fps	40.5 grains	3300 fps	22" barrel, 1:9"
Lyman	36.3 grains	3164 fps	40.5 grains	3457 fps	24" barrel, 1:9"
Sierra	38.8 grains	3000 fps	40.3 grains	3100 fps	22" barrel, 1:9"

*The Barnes and Speer manuals do not list Varget powder for the 75-grain bullet. The Nosler manual does not list a 75-grain bullet.

Hodgdon VARGET Powder—80-Grain Bullet*

Manual	Minimum Charge	Muzzle Velocity	Maximum Charge	Muzzle Velocity	Barrel Length, Twist Rate
Hornady	34.1 grains	2800 fps	41.0 grains	3300 fps	22" barrel, 1:9"
Lyman	35.4 grains	3188 fps	39.6 grains	3364 fps	24" barrel, 1:9"
Nosler	38.0 grains	3121 fps	42.0 grains	3384 fps	24" barrel, 1:10"
Sierra	36.4 grains	2800 fps	40.0 grains	3100 fps	22" barrel, 1:9"

*The Barnes manual does not list an 80-grain bullet. The Speer manual does not list Varget powder for the 80-grain bullet.

Note: Only the Nosler and Sierra manuals list a 55-grain bullet, and neither lists N140 powder.

Vihtavuori N140 Powder—58/60/62 Grain-Bullets*

Manual	Minimum Charge	Muzzle Velocity	Maximum Charge	Muzzle Velocity	Barrel Length, Twist Rate
Hornady	41.4 grains	3300 fps	45.2 grains	3700 fps	22" barrel, 1:9" twist, 58-grain bullet
Lyman	38.5 grains	3328 fps	43.0 grains	3673 fps	24" barrel, 1:9" twist, 60-grain bullet

*The Barnes manual does not list N140 powder for its 62-grain bullet. The Nosler and Speer manuals do not list a 58-, 60-, or 62-grain bullet. The Sierra manual does not list N140 powder for its 60-grain bullet.

Vihtavuori N140 Powder—65-Grain Bullet*

Manual	Minimum Charge	Muzzle Velocity	Maximum Charge	Muzzle Velocity	Barrel Length, Twist Rate
Hornady	38.4 grains	3100 fps	43.2 grains	3500 fps	22" barrel, 1:9"

*Only the Hornady manual lists a 65-grain bullet.

Vihtavuori N140 Powder—70-Grain Bullet*

Manual	Minimum Charge	Muzzle Velocity	Maximum Charge	Muzzle Velocity	Barrel Length, Twist Rate
Hornady	36.6 grains	2900 fps	42.2 grains	3300 fps	22" barrel, 1:9"
Lyman	37.0 grains	3248 fps	42.3 grains	3530 fps	24" barrel, 1:9"
Sierra	39.1 grains	3000 fps	42.7 grains	3300 fps	22" barrel, 1:9"

*The Barnes manual does not list a 70-grain bullet. The Nosler and Speer manuals do not list N140 powder for the 70-grain bullet.

Vihtavuori N140 Powder—75-Grain Bullet*

Manual	Minimum Charge	Muzzle Velocity	Maximum Charge	Muzzle Velocity	Barrel Length, Twist Rate
Hornady	37.0 grains	2900 fps	41.7 grains	3200 fps	22" barrel, 1:9"
Lyman	36.7 grains	3092 fps	41.0 grains	3398 fps	24" barrel, 1:9"
Sierra	39.1 grains	3000 fps	42.7 grains	3300 fps	22" barrel, 1:9"
Speer	39.0 grains	2999 fps	43.0 grains	3293 fps	24" barrel

*The Barnes manual does not list N140 powder for the 75-grain bullet. The Nosler manual does not list a 75-grain bullet.

Vihtavuori N140 Powder—80-Grain Bullet*

Manual	Minimum Charge	Muzzle Velocity	Maximum Charge	Muzzle Velocity	Barrel Length, Twist Rate
Hornady	35.5 grains	2800 fps	41.8 grains	3200 fps	22" barrel, 1:9"
Lyman	35.8 grains	3044 fps	40.0 grains	3301 fps	24" barrel, 1:9"
Sierra	37.0 grains	2800 fps	41.2 grains	3100 fps	22" barrel, 1:9"

*The Barnes manual does not list an 80-grain bullet. The Nosler and Speer manuals do not list N140 powder for the 80-grain bullet.

RANGE TESTS

On the day I tested the 6mm Remington, the weather was mostly sunny with a variable wind from 6 o'clock; the temperature was in the mid-70s. For factory ammo, I chose the Federal 80-grain soft point ammunition. The test results can be seen on the next page and are as follows:

Group 1 measured 2.29" center to center with four of the shots in 1.5". Group 2 measured 1.28" center to center with four of the shots in 1.01". I consider this reasonably good accuracy for factory ammunition.

The average velocity, as measured by the Oehler chronograph, was 3369 fps for the Federal factory ammo. This is quite close to the 3400 fps listed by Federal for its 80-grain bullet.

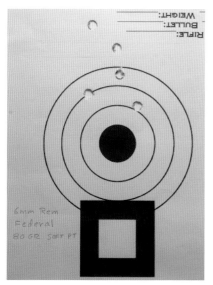

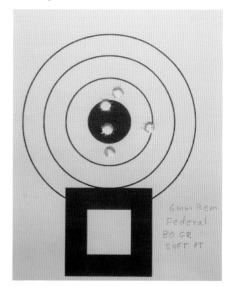

6mm Remington—Factory Ammo Group 1.

6mm Remington—Factory Ammo Group 2.

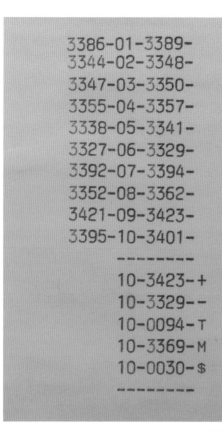

The Oehler chronograph data for Federal's 80-grain factory ammunition indicates an average velocity (M) of 3369 fps and a standard deviation ($) of 30 fps.

This low standard deviation reading indicates consistent ammo.

```
3386-01-3389-
3344-02-3348-
3347-03-3350-
3355-04-3357-
3338-05-3341-
3327-06-3329-
3392-07-3394-
3352-08-3362-
3421-09-3423-
3395-10-3401-
--------
10-3423-+
10-3329--
10-0094-T
10-3369-M
10-0030-$
--------
```

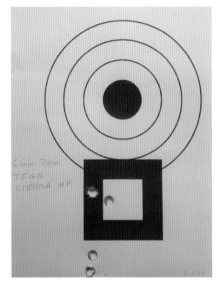

6mm Remington—Handload Group 1.

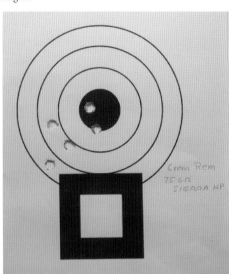

6mm Remington—Handload Group 2.

The 6mm Remington handload that I tested—Sierra 75-grain hollow point bullet, 44.5 grains of IMR 4350 powder, and the CCI 200 primer—produced the following five-shot groups.

The first group measured 1.84" (the highest shot is a double), and the second group measured 1.56" with the upper four shots in 1.02".

The chronograph measured an average velocity of 3038 fps for my handload. This agrees closely with the data provided by Sierra.

While both the factory ammunition and my handload produced reasonable accuracy for an untuned Ruger No. 1, I believe it's possible to achieve MOA accuracy with this rifle and plan to continue load development with this as my goal.

```
3048-01-3045-
2982-02-2979-
3069-03-3066-
3074-04-3072-
2967-05-2965-
3108-06-3101-
3032-07-3028-
3007-08-3000-
3079-09-3071-
3069-10-3061-
---------
10-3101-+
10-2965--
10-0136-T
10-3038-M
10-0044-$
---------
```

For the 6mm Remington handload, the chronograph measured an average velocity (M) of 3038 fps and a standard deviation (S) of 44 fps.

This average velocity agrees with the data in the various reloading manuals.

TRAJECTORY TABLES

The following trajectory tables were developed using the Handloads.com ballistic calculator. The tables are based on the line of sight (LOS) being 1.5 inches above the line of fire (LOF). All tabular data is expressed in inches.

55-Grain Bullet (BC = .225)

Muzzle Velocity (fps)	Muzzle	100 yards	200 yards	300 yards	400 yards
	−1.5	0.0	−1.4	−6.7	−17.3
4000	−1.5	0.7	0.0	−4.6	−14.5
	−1.5	2.2	3.1	0.0	−8.3
	−1.5	0.0	−1.6	−7.3	−18.5
3900	−1.5	0.8	0.0	−4.9	−15.3
	−1.5	2.4	3.3	0.0	−8.8
	−1.5	0.0	−1.7	−7.8	−20.0
3800	−1.5	0.9	0.0	−5.2	−16.3
	−1.5	2.6	3.5	0.0	−9.4
	−1.5	0.0	−1.9	−8.5	−21.2
3700	−1.5	1.0	0.0	−5.6	−17.4
	−1.5	2.8	3.7	0.0	−10.0
	−1.5	0.0	−2.1	−9.1	−22.8
3600	−1.5	1.1	0.0	−5.9	−18.5
	−1.5	3.0	4.0	0.0	−10.6
	−1.5	0.0	−2.3	−9.9	−24.5
3500	−1.5	1.2	0.0	−6.4	−19.8
	−1.5	3.3	4.2	0.0	−11.4
	−1.5	0.0	−2.6	−10.7	−26.0
3400	−1.5	1.3	0.0	−6.8	−21.2
	−1.5	3.6	4.6	0.0	−12.2
	−1.5	0.0	−2.8	−11.6	−28.5
3300	−1.5	1.4	0.0	−7.3	−22.8
	−1.5	3.9	4.9	0.0	−13.0

6mm Remington

60-Grain Bullet (BC = .250)

Muzzle Velocity (fps)	Muzzle	100 yards	200 yards	300 yards	400 yards
	−1.5	0.0	−1.5	−6.8	−17.2
3900	−1.5	0.7	0.0	−4.6	−14.3
	−1.5	2.3	3.1	0.0	−8.1
	−1.5	0.0	−1.7	−7.4	−18.4
3800	−1.5	0.8	0.0	−4.9	−15.2
	−1.5	2.5	3.3	0.0	−8.6
	−1.5	0.0	−1.8	−8.0	−19.8
3700	−1.5	0.9	0.0	−5.2	−16.1
	−1.5	2.7	3.5	0.0	−9.2
	−1.5	0.0	−2.0	−8.6	−21.2
3600	−1.5	1.0	0.0	−5.6	−17.2
	−1.5	2.9	3.7	0.0	−9.8
	−1.5	0.0	−2.2	−9.3	−22.8
3500	−1.5	1.1	0.0	−6.0	−18.4
	−1.5	3.1	4.0	0.0	−10.4
	−1.5	0.0	−2.5	−10.1	−24.6
3400	−1.5	1.2	0.0	−6.4	−19.7
	−1.5	3.4	4.3	0.0	−11.1
	−1.5	0.0	−2.7	−10.9	−26.5
3300	−1.5	1.4	0.0	−6.9	−21.1
	−1.5	3.7	4.6	0.0	−12.0
	−1.5	0.0	−3.0	−11.9	−28.7
3200	−1.5	1.5	0.0	−7.4	−22.7
	−1.5	4.0	4.9	0.0	−12.8

123

65-Grain Bullet (BC = .280)

Muzzle Velocity (fps)	Muzzle	100 yards	200 yards	300 yards	400 yards
	−1.5	0.0	−1.7	−7.5	−18.5
3700	−1.5	0.9	0.0	−4.9	−15.0
	−1.5	2.5	3.3	0.0	−8.5
	−1.5	0.0	−1.9	−8.1	−19.9
3600	−1.5	1.0	0.0	−5.3	−16.0
	−1.5	2.7	3.5	0.0	−9.0
	−1.5	0.0	−2.1	−8.8	−21.4
3500	−1.5	1.1	0.0	−5.6	−17.1
	−1.5	2.9	3.8	0.0	−9.6
	−1.5	0.0	−2.3	−9.5	−23.0
3400	−1.5	1.2	0.0	−6.0	−18.3
	−1.5	3.2	4.0	0.0	−10.3
	−1.5	0.0	−2.6	−10.4	−24.8
3300	−1.5	1.3	0.0	−6.5	−19.7
	−1.5	3.5	4.3	0.0	−11.0
	−1.5	0.0	−2.9	−11.3	−26.8
3200	−1.5	1.4	0.0	−7.0	−21.1
	−1.5	3.8	4.7	0.0	−11.8
	−1.5	0.0	−3.1	−12.2	−29.0
3100	−1.5	1.6	0.0	−7.5	−22.7
	−1.5	4.1	5.0	0.0	−12.7

70-Grain Bullet (BC = .270)

Muzzle Velocity (fps)	Muzzle	100 yards	200 yards	300 yards	400 yards
	−1.5	0.0	−1.9	−8.3	−20.3
3600	−1.5	1.0	0.0	−5.4	−16.4
	−1.5	2.8	3.6	0.0	−9.2
	−1.5	0.0	−2.1	−9.0	−21.8
3500	−1.5	1.1	0.0	−5.7	−17.5
	−1.5	3.0	3.8	0.0	−9.9
	−1.5	0.0	−2.4	−9.7	−23.5
3400	−1.5	1.2	0.0	−6.2	−18.7
	−1.5	3.2	4.1	0.0	−10.5
	−1.5	0.0	−2.6	−10.5	−25.3
3300	−1.5	1.3	0.0	−6.6	−20.1
	−1.5	3.5	4.4	0.0	−11.3
	−1.5	0.0	−2.9	−11.4	−27.4
3200	−1.5	1.4	0.0	−7.1	−21.6
	−1.5	3.8	4.7	0.0	−12.1
	−1.5	0.0	−3.2	−12.4	−29.7
3100	−1.5	1.6	0.0	−7.7	−23.3
	−1.5	4.1	5.1	0.0	−13.1
	−1.5	0.0	−3.5	−13.6	−32.2
3000	−1.5	1.8	0.0	−8.3	−25.1
	−1.5	4.5	5.5	0.0	−14.1

75-Grain Bullet (BC = .300)

Muzzle Velocity (fps)	Muzzle	100 yards	200 yards	300 yards	400 yards
	−1.5	0.0	−2.3	−9.3	−22.2
3400	−1.5	1.1	0.0	−5.9	−17.6
	−1.5	3.1	3.9	0.0	−9.8
	−1.5	0.0	−2.5	−10.1	−23.9
3300	−1.5	1.3	0.0	−6.3	−18.9
	−1.5	3.4	4.2	0.0	−10.5
	−1.5	0.0	−2.8	−10.9	−28.9
3200	−1.5	1.4	0.0	−6.8	−20.3
	−1.5	3.6	4.5	0.0	−11.3
	−1.5	0.0	−3.1	−11.9	−28.0
3100	−1.5	1.5	0.0	−7.3	−21.9
	−1.5	4.0	4.9	0.0	−12.1
	−1.5	0.0	−3.4	−12.9	−30.4
3000	−1.5	1.7	0.0	−7.9	−23.6
	−1.5	4.3	5.2	0.0	−13.1
	−1.5	0.0	−3.7	−14.1	−33.0
2900	−1.5	1.9	0.0	−8.5	−25.5
	−1.5	4.7	5.7	0.0	−14.2

80-Grain Bullet (BC = .320)

Muzzle Velocity (fps)	Muzzle	100 yards	200 yards	300 yards	400 yards
	−1.5	0.0	−2.2	−9.0	−21.5
3400	−1.5	1.1	0.0	−5.7	−17.0
	−1.5	3.0	3.8	0.0	−9.5
	−1.5	0.0	−2.5	−9.8	−23.2
3300	−1.5	1.2	0.0	−6.1	−18.3
	−1.5	3.3	4.1	0.0	−10.1
	−1.5	0.0	−2.7	−10.6	−25.0
3200	−1.5	1.4	0.0	−6.6	−19.6
	−1.5	3.6	4.4	0.0	−10.9
	−1.5	0.0	−3.0	−11.6	−27.1
3100	−1.5	1.5	0.0	−7.1	−21.1
	−1.5	3.9	4.7	0.0	−11.7
	−1.5	0.0	−3.3	−12.6	−29.4
3000	−1.5	1.7	0.0	−7.6	−22.8
	−1.5	4.2	5.1	0.0	−12.6
	−1.5	0.0	−3.7	−13.8	−31.9
2900	−1.5	1.8	0.0	−8.3	−24.6
	−1.5	4.6	5.5	0.0	−13.6
	−1.5	0.0	−4.1	−15.1	−34.8
2800	−1.5	2.0	0.0	−9.0	−26.7
	−1.5	5.0	6.0	0.0	−14.7

Chapter 9
.257 Roberts

C redit for the development of the .257 Roberts belongs to Ned H. Roberts, a well-known experimenter and gun writer from the 1920s and '30s. His wildcat was created by necking the 7×57mm Mauser cartridge down to .25 caliber. In 1934, Remington, released the .257 Roberts as a factory round. The only change made was to alter the shoulder angle from 15 to 20 degrees.

The .257 Roberts was quickly accepted by the shooting fraternity as a combination varmint and medium-sized game cartridge. Its popularity was demonstrated by the fact that all the major firearms manufacturers at that time offered this chambering in one or more of their rifles. The Roberts remained popular as a dual-purpose cartridge until 1955, when it was unseated by both the .243 Winchester and the .244 Remington. The .257 Roberts was underloaded at that time, and the factory cartridges only offered 100- and 117-grain blunt-nosed bullets. It also faced stiff competition in 1969 when Remington commercialized the .25-06.

None of this changes the fact that the .257 Roberts, when handloaded with 75-grain varmint bullets to velocities approaching 3400 fps, makes for an excellent varmint cartridge. To my knowledge, the only factory rifles currently chambered for this fine cartridge are those made by Kimber, Ruger, and Winchester.

THE RUGER MODEL 77 HAWKEYE

The Ruger Model 77 Hawkeye is a fairly new version of the firm's Model 77 center-fire bolt-action rifle and was first introduced in 2006. The Hawkeye features an American walnut stock with a slim rounded profile and wraparound hand checkering on the fore-end. With a 22 inch sporter barrel in .257 Roberts, this rifle is ideally suited as a walking-around varmint rifle. The rifling twist for the .257 Roberts is 1:10".

One new feature of the Hawkeye that I do not accept is the LC6 trigger. While the trigger was smooth and crisp, the four-plus pound weight was, in my opinion, too heavy for use as a varmint rifle. I replaced the factory trigger with a Spec-Tech trigger that I was able to safely adjust to a clean, crisp pull of one and three-fourths pounds.

The scope is a variable power Leupold VX-2 3-9×40mm with the Duplex reticle and $\frac{1}{4}$ MOA windage and elevation adjustments. The scope is mounted using the Ruger rings that were included with the rifle.

With its 22-inch sporter barrel and slim forearm, the Hawkeye, in combination with its scope and mounts, weighs slightly less than nine pounds.

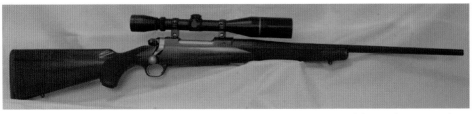

Author's Ruger Model 77 Hawkeye—.257 Roberts.

.257 ROBERTS FACTORY AMMO

Currently, there is no factory ammunition available for the .257 Roberts cartridge that is suitable for varmint hunting. The lightest bullet weight available in a factory offering is the +P 110-grain AccuBond from Nosler. This means that if you wish to consider the .257 Roberts for varmint shooting, handloading is the only way to go.

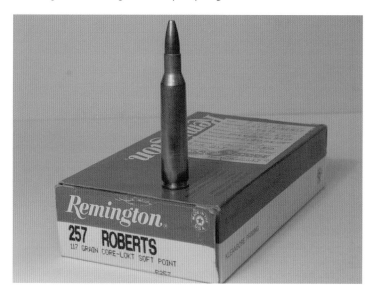

The .257 Roberts, while not as popular as the .243 Winchester and 6mm Remington, is still a fine dual-purpose cartridge for both varmints and medium-size game, such as deer and antelope.

For varmint shooting, however, handloading is your only option.

HANDLOADING THE .257 ROBERTS

Because there is currently no .257 Roberts factory ammunition suitable for varmint hunting, handloading is the only option. Fortunately, .257 Roberts brass is readily available, and all the major reloading manuals offer loads for this cartridge. Also, all the latest reloading manuals caution that the loads listed are designed for +P pressures in the .257 Roberts and should only be used in modern firearms designed for this cartridge.

Barnes Reloading Manual Number 4

The Barnes manual lists loads for its 90-, 100-, and 115-grain bullets. However, I think that 90 grains is about the upper limit I would consider for a varmint round in the .257 Roberts.

For the 90-grain Barnes BND SPIT bullet, Reloder 19 powder produced the best accuracy.

Hornady Handbook of Cartridge Reloading, 8th Edition

Hornady includes +P loads for its 60-, 75-, and 87-grain bullets. The Hornady manual does not specifically mention any powders that produced the best accuracy in the .257 Roberts for any of the company's bullets.

Lyman Reloading Handbook, 49th Edition

The Lyman manual lists .257 Roberts loads for bullet weights from 75 to 117 grains. For developing varmint loads, we will consider the load data for the 75- and 87-grain bullets. Lyman recommends Alliant Reloder 15 powder for the 75-grain bullet, and Hodgdon's Varget for the 87-grain bullet.

128

Nosler Reloading Guide No. 6

Nosler lists loads for its 85-, 100-, 110-, 115-, and 120-grain 6mm bullets. For varmint loads for the .257 Roberts, we will only consider the data for the 85-grain bullet. The most accurate load tested by Nosler was obtained using Reloder 15 powder.

Sierra 5th Edition Reloading Manual

Sierra includes load tables for its 75-, 87-, 90-, 100-, and 117-grain bullets. We will only consider the loads for the 75-, 87-, and 90-grain bullets, as they are applicable to varmint shooting.

Sierra's accuracy load for the 75-grain bullet was with 48 grains of Accurate's AA4350 powder; for hunting, 44.7 grains of IMR 4320. The best accuracy for the Sierra 87- and 90-grain bullets was obtained using Varget powder. The

best hunting load was obtained using Reloder 15 powder.

Speer Reloading Manual #14

The Speer manual includes .257 Roberts loads for its 75-, 87-, 100-, 115-, and 120-grain bullets. For varmint shooting applications, we will only list data for the 75- and 87-grain bullets. Speer lists many of the powders that most of the other manuals also include, but does not identify any powders as producing the best accuracy. Also, the Speer manual does not list the twist rate for its .257 Roberts test firearm barrel.

The following tables list some loads from the current reloading manuals for each bullet weight from 75 to 90 grains. I consider these weights suitable for varmint shooting with the .257 Roberts.

IMR 4895 Powder—75-Grain Bullet*

Manual	Minimum Charge	Muzzle Velocity	Maximum Charge	Muzzle Velocity	Barrel Length, Twist Rate
Lyman	38.0 grains	2890 fps	42.0 grains	3268 fps	24" barrel, 1:10"
Sierra	38.3 grains	3000 fps	43.8 grains	3300 fps	22" barrel, 1:10"
Speer	37.0 grains	2772 fps	41.0 grains	3157 fps	24" barrel

*The Barnes and Nosler manuals do not list a 75-grain bullet. The Hornady manual does not list IMR 4895 powder for its 75-grain bullet.

IMR 4895 Powder—85-Grain Bullet*

Manual	Minimum Charge	Muzzle Velocity	Maximum Charge	Muzzle Velocity	Barrel Length, Twist Rate
Nosler	38.0 grains	3042 fps	42.0 grains	3352 fps	24" barrel, 1:10"

*Only Nosler lists data for an 85-grain bullet.

IMR 4895 Powder—87/90-Grain Bullets*

Manual	Minimum Charge	Muzzle Velocity	Maximum Charge	Muzzle Velocity	Barrel Length, Twist Rate
Lyman	36.0 grains	2724 fps	40.0 grains	3030 fps	24" barrel, 1:10" twist, 87-grain bullet
Sierra	35.3 grains	2800 fps	40.8 grains	3200 fps	22" barrel, 1:10" twist, 87/90-grain bullets

*The Barnes, Hornady, and Speer manuals do not list IMR 4895 powder for their 87/90-grain bullets. The Nosler manual does not list an 87- or 90-grain bullet.

IMR 4350 Powder—75-Grain Bullet*

Manual	Minimum Charge	Muzzle Velocity	Maximum Charge	Muzzle Velocity	Barrel Length, Twist Rate
Hornady	40.9 grains	3000 fps	49.1 grains	3500 fps	22" barrel, 1:10"
Lyman	45.0 grains	2728 fps	47.0 grains	2963 fps	24" barrel, 1:10"
Sierra	43.8 grains	3000 fps	49.4 grains	3400 fps	22" barrel, 1:9"
Speer	45.0 grains	2895 fps	49.0 grains	3265 fps	24" barrel

*The Barnes and Nosler manuals do not list a 75-grain bullet. The Lyman and Sierra manuals list AA4350 powder, which is equivalent to IMR 4350 powder.

IMR 4350 Powder—85-Grain Bullet*

Manual	Minimum Charge	Muzzle Velocity	Maximum Charge	Muzzle Velocity	Barrel Length, Twist Rate
Nosler	43.5 grains	2902 fps	47.5 grains	3272 fps	24" barrel, 1:10"

*Only Nosler lists data for an 85-grain bullet.

IMR 4350 Powder—87/90-Grain Bullets*

Manual	Minimum Charge	Muzzle Velocity	Maximum Charge	Muzzle Velocity	Barrel Length, Twist Rate
Barnes	43.0 grains	2984 fps	47.0 grains	3267 fps	24" barrel, 1:10" twist, 90-grain bullet
Hornady	37.8 grains	2800 fps	45.6 grains	3200 fps	22" barrel, 1:10" twist, 87-grain bullet
Lyman	43.0 grains	2642 fps	45.5 grains	2814 fps	24" barrel, 1:10" twist, 87-grain bullet
Sierra	41.1 grains	2800 fps	47.1 grains	3300 fps	22" barrel, 1:10" twist, 87/90-grain bullets
Speer	43.0 grains	2876 fps	47.0 grains	3069 fps	24" barrel, 87-grain bullet

*The Lyman manual lists AA4350 powder, which is equivalent to IMR 4350 powder. The Nosler manual does not list an 87- or 90-grain bullet. The Sierra Manual lists H4350 EXT, which has a slightly different burning rate than IMR 4350 powder.

IMR 4064 Powder—75-Grain Bullet*

Manual	Minimum Charge	Muzzle Velocity	Maximum Charge	Muzzle Velocity	Barrel Length, Twist Rate
Hornady	35.3 grains	3000 fps	43.3 grains	3400 fps	22" barrel, 1:10"
Lyman	40.0 grains	3012 fps	44.0 grains	3509 fps	24" barrel, 1:10"
Sierra	38.9 grains	3000 fps	44.1 grains	3500 fps	22" barrel, 1:10"
Speer	38.0 grains	2795 fps	42.0 grains	3126 fps	24" barrel

*The Barnes and Nosler manuals do not list a 75-grain bullet.

IMR 4064 Powder—85-Grain Bullet*

Manual	Minimum Charge	Muzzle Velocity	Maximum Charge	Muzzle Velocity	Barrel Length, Twist Rate
Nosler	39.5 grains	3060 fps	43.5 grains	3360 fps	24" barrel, 1:10"

*Only Nosler lists data for an 85-grain bullet.

IMR 4064 Powder—87/90-Grain Bullets*

Manual	Minimum Charge	Muzzle Velocity	Maximum Charge	Muzzle Velocity	Barrel Length, Twist Rate
Hornady	33.6 grains	2800 fps	42.2 grains	3300 fps	22" barrel, 1:10" twist, 87-grain bullet
Lyman	39.0 grains	2932 fps	43.0 grains	3311 fps	24" barrel, 1:10" twist, 87-grain bullet
Sierra	36.1 grains	2800 fps	42.1 grains	3300 fps	22" barrel, 1:10" twist, 87/90-grain bullets

*The Barnes manual does not list IMR 4064 powder for its 90-grain bullet. The Nosler manual does not list an 87- or 90-grain bullet. The Speer manual does not list IMR 4064 powder for its 87-grain bullet.

Hodgdon VARGET Powder—75-Grain Bullet*

Manual	Minimum Charge	Muzzle Velocity	Maximum Charge	Muzzle Velocity	Barrel Length, Twist Rate
Hornady	33.7 grains	3000 fps	43.1 grains	3500 fps	22" barrel, 1:10"
Lyman	39.0 grains	2920 fps	41.0 grains	3084 fps	24" barrel, 1:10"
Sierra	40.1 grains	3000 fps	41.7 grains	3200 fps	22" barrel, 1:10"

*The Barnes and Nosler manuals do not list a 75-grain bullet.

Hodgdon VARGET Powder—85-Grain Bullet*

Manual	Minimum Charge	Muzzle Velocity	Maximum Charge	Muzzle Velocity	Barrel Length, Twist Rate
Nosler	37.0 grains	3015 fps	41.0 grains	3226 fps	24" barrel, 1:10"

*Only Nosler lists data for an 85-grain bullet.

Hodgdon VARGET Powder—87/90-Grain Bullets*

Manual	Minimum Charge	Muzzle Velocity	Maximum Charge	Muzzle Velocity	Barrel Length, Twist Rate
Hornady	34.3 grains	2800 fps	38.4 grains	3100 fps	22" barrel, 1:10" twist, 87-grain bullet
Lyman	38.0 grains	2893 fps	40.2 grains	3029 fps	24" barrel, 1:10" twist, 87-grain bullet
Sierra	36.8 grains	2800 fps	40.7 grains	3100 fps	22" barrel, 1:10" twist, 87/90-grain bullets

*The Barnes manual does not list Varget powder for its 90-grain bullet. The Nosler manual does not list an 87- or 90-grain bullet. The Speer manual does not list Varget powder for its 87-grain bullet.

Alliant Reloder 15 Powder—75-Grain Bullet*

Manual	Minimum Charge	Muzzle Velocity	Maximum Charge	Muzzle Velocity	Barrel Length, Twist Rate
Hornady	36.3 grains	3000 fps	43.1 grains	3400 fps	22" barrel, 1:10"
Lyman	39.0 grains	2967 fps	41.8 grains	3190 fps	24" barrel, 1:10"
Sierra	39.2 grains	3000 fps	41.4 grains	3200 fps	22" barrel, 1:10"
Speer	39.0 grains	2852 fps	43.0 grains	3223 fps	24" barrel

*The Barnes and Nosler manuals do not list a 75-grain bullet.

Alliant Reloder 15—85-Grain Bullet*

Manual	Minimum Charge	Muzzle Velocity	Maximum Charge	Muzzle Velocity	Barrel Length, Twist Rate
Nosler	39.5 grains	3082 fps	43.5 grains	3381 fps	24" barrel, 1:10"

*Only Nosler lists data for an 85-grain bullet.

Alliant Reloder 15—87/90-Grain Bullets*

Manual	Minimum Charge	Muzzle Velocity	Maximum Charge	Muzzle Velocity	Barrel Length, Twist Rate
Hornady	34.4 grains	2800 fps	41.5 grains	3200 fps	22" barrel, 1:10" twist, 87-grain bullet
Lyman	39.0 grains	2953 fps	41.0 grains	3101 fps	24" barrel, 1:10" twist, 87-grain bullet
Sierra	36.2 grains	2800 fps	40.4 grains	3100 fps	22" barrel, 1:10" twist, 87/90-grain bullets
Speer	39.0 grains	2804 fps	43.0 grains	3129 fps	24" barrel

*The Barnes manual does not list RL 15 powder for its 90-grain bullet. The Nosler manual does not list an 87- or 90-grain bullet.

RANGE TESTS

The day that I tested the .257 Roberts had a mostly sunny sky, a moderate wind from 6 o'clock, and a temperature in the mid-70s. For the .257 Roberts hand load, I chose the Sierra 75-grain HP bullet, 42 grains of IMR 4064 powder, and the CCI 200 primer.

Group 1 measured 1.52" center to center; group 2, 1.47" center to center. This is acceptable accuracy for a dual-purpose varmint and medium-game rifle. I think that with some additional load experimentation, I can shrink the average group size to about 1 MOA. Also, this is a fairly new rifle with only a little over one hundred rounds down the tube, so the barrel is probably not fully broken in yet.

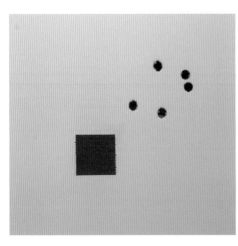

.257 Roberts—Handload Group 1.

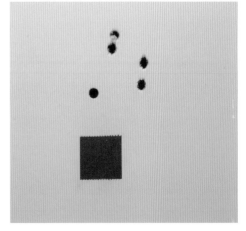

.257 Roberts—Handload Group 2.

The average velocity measured by my Oehler chronograph was 2992 fps. This is about 300 fps lower than the 3300 fps listed by Sierra for its 75-grain bullet and 42 grains of IMR 4064 powder. The Speer manual lists this load as a maximum charge, but there was no indication of high pressure.

```
3014-01-3018-
2973-02-2977-
2969-03-2973-
2967-04-2970-
2987-05-2990-
2987-06-2988-
2952-07-2952-
3012-08-3010-
3055-09-3055-
2989-10-2989-

---------

10-3055-+
10-2952--
10-0103-T
10-2992-M
10-0029-$

---------
```

The average velocity (M) measured by the Oehler Model 35P was 2992 fps, and the standard deviation ($) was 26 fps. This is about 300 fps lower than that shown in the Sierra manual for its 75-grain bullet, but only about 100 fps slower than the Speer manual data for the 75-grain bullet. In fact, according to the Speer data, 42 grains of IMR 4064 powder is a maximum charge.

This handload is quite consistent, as indicated by the low standard deviation number.

TRAJECTORY TABLES

The following trajectory tables were developed using the Handloads.com ballistic calculator. The tables are based on the line of sight (LOS) being 1.5 inches above the line of fire (LOF). All tabular data is expressed in inches.

75-Grain Bullet (BC = .290)

Muzzle Velocity (fps)	Muzzle	100 yards	200 yards	300 yards	400 yards
	−1.5	0.0	−2.1	−8.7	−21.0
3500	−1.5	1.0	0.0	−5.6	−16.8
	−1.5	2.9	3.7	0.0	−9.4
	−1.5	0.0	−2.3	−9.4	−22.6
3400	−1.5	1.2	0.0	−5.9	−18.0
	−1.5	3.1	4.0	0.0	−10.0
	−1.5	0.0	−2.5	−10.2	−24.4
3300	−1.5	1.3	0.0	−6.4	−19.3
	−1.5	3.4	4.3	0.0	−10.8
	−1.5	0.0	−2.8	−11.1	−26.3
3200	−1.5	1.4	0.0	−6.9	−20.7
	−1.5	3.7	4.6	0.0	−11.5
	−1.5	0.0	−3.1	−12.1	−28.5
3100	−1.5	1.6	0.0	−7.4	−22.3
	−1.5	4.0	4.9	0.0	−12.4
	−1.5	0.0	−3.4	−13.1	−30.9
3000	−1.5	1.7	0.0	−8.0	−24.0
	−1.5	4.4	5.3	0.0	−13.4
	−1.5	0.0	−3.8	−14.3	−33.6
2900	−1.5	1.9	0.0	−8.7	−26.0
	−1.5	4.8	5.8	0.0	−14.5
	−1.5	0.0	−4.2	−15.7	−36.6
2800	−1.5	2.1	0.0	−9.4	−28.2
	−1.5	5.2	6.3	0.0	−15.7
	−1.5	0.0	−4.7	−17.2	−40.0
2700	−1.5	2.3	0.0	−10.2	−30.7
	−1.5	5.7	6.8	0.0	−17.1

85-Grain Bullet (BC = .330)

Muzzle Velocity (fps)	Muzzle	100 yards	200 yards	300 yards	400 yards
	−1.5	0.0	−2.2	−8.9	−21.2
3400	−1.5	1.1	0.0	−5.6	−16.8
	−1.5	3.0	3.7	0.0	−9.3
	−1.5	0.0	−2.4	−9.7	−22.8
3300	−1.5	1.2	0.0	−6.0	−18.0
	−1.5	3.2	4.0	0.0	−10.0
	−1.5	0.0	−2.7	−10.5	−24.7
3200	−1.5	1.3	0.0	−6.5	−19.3
	−1.5	3.5	4.3	0.0	−10.7
	−1.5	0.0	−3.0	−11.4	−26.7
3100	−1.5	1.5	0.0	−7.0	−20.8
	−1.5	3.8	4.7	0.0	−11.5
	−1.5	0.0	−3.3	−13.5	−29.0
3000	−1.5	1.6	0.0	−7.5	−22.3
	−1.5	4.2	5.0	0.0	−12.4
	−1.5	0.0	−3.6	−13.6	−31.5
2900	−1.5	1.8	0.0	−8.2	−24.2
	−1.5	4.5	5.4	0.0	−13.4

87/90-Grain Bullet (BC = .320)

Muzzle Velocity (fps)	Muzzle	100 yards	200 yards	300 yards	400 yards
	−1.5	0.0	−2.5	−9.8	−23.2
3300	−1.5	1.2	0.0	−6.1	−18.3
	−1.5	3.3	4.1	0.0	−10.1
	−1.5	0.0	−2.7	−10.6	−25.0
3200	−1.5	1.4	0.0	−6.6	−19.6
	−1.5	3.6	4.4	0.0	−10.9
	−1.5	0.0	−3.0	−11.6	−27.1
3100	−1.5	1.5	0.0	−7.1	−21.1
	−1.5	3.9	4.7	0.0	−11.7
	−1.5	0.0	−3.3	−12.6	−29.4
3000	−1.5	1.7	0.0	−7.6	−22.8
	−1.5	4.2	5.1	0.0	−12.6
	−1.5	0.0	−3.7	−13.8	−31.9
2900	−1.5	1.8	0.0	−8.3	−24.6
	−1.5	4.6	5.5	0.0	−13.6
	−1.5	0.0	−4.1	−15.1	−34.8
2800	−1.5	2.0	0.0	−9.0	−26.7
	−1.5	5.0	6.0	0.0	−14.7
	−1.5	0.0	−4.5	−16.5	−38.0
2700	−1.5	2.2	0.0	−9.8	−29.0
	−1.5	5.5	6.5	0.0	−16.0

Some Parting Thoughts

I have many pleasant memories of times spent at the edge of an alfalfa field with my back to the woods. The only sounds I could hear were the insects buzzing around and an occasional bird chirping. Looking toward the sky, I could sometimes view a hawk circling around looking for its lunch. This is what it was like to hunt woodchucks in northern New Jersey in the 1970s. There were a few large dairy farms where I had established a good relationship with the farmer, who was happy to have me get rid of some of those pesky woodchucks.

I waited until early June after the first mowing for two reasons. First, the chucks were easier to spot in the short grass; second, the young ones had been weaned from their mothers and could now survive on their own. I would glass the sloping field with my binoculars until I spotted one of the little creatures moving away from its den, and then I would carefully lie down in the prone position and wrap my arm in the military sling—bipods weren't that popular yet. Once the crosshairs had settled on the target and my breathing was relaxed, I let off the shot and listened for the *plop* sound that would indicate he was a goner! Contrast this experience with being on a deer stand during the frigid month of December waiting for a buck to appear, and you will understand why I enjoyed woodchuck hunting so much.

Now let me ramble on about some other topics that may or may not be related to varmint shooting. Why is it that some great cartridges have been relegated to the dust bin? I'll start with the fine little .222 Remington. This is the same cartridge that sired the .221 Fireball, .222 Remington Magnum, .223 Remington, and .204 Ruger. I can understand, to some extent, how after being chosen as the new 5.56×47mm NATO round, the .223 Remington nudged the .222 Remington Magnum aside. But it now seems that the .223 Remington and .204 Ruger have ganged up on the .222 Remington and pushed it to near obsolescence.

On a visit to my local sporting goods store, I struck up a conversation with one of the salesmen behind the counter in the gun department. We began discussing this very topic—why many good cartridges seem to fade away. He showed me a nice little CZ 527 American chambered for the .222 Remington and said that it had been sitting there on the rack for quite some time. Even though the .223 Remington and .204 Ruger are currently popular, it does not change the fact that the .222 Remington, their progenitor, is still a great varmint cartridge. Its inherent accuracy can be attested to by how long it was a favorite of the benchrest fraternity. To my knowledge, the only factory rifles currently chambered for the triple deuce are the CZ Model 527, Sako Model 85, Savage Model 25, and Tikka T3. How sad!

Other excellent cartridges that are, for the most part, nearly obsolete, are the standard 7×57mm Mauser and its descendants, the .257 Roberts and 6mm Remington. I'll start with the 7mm Mauser, which was developed way back in 1892 and proved its worth against us in Cuba during the Spanish-American War. I'm sure that one factor contributing to its loss in popularity was the appearance of such cartridges as the 7mm Remington Magnum, 7mm-08, .280 Remington, and .284 Winchester. While these are all fine cartridges, a handloaded 7mm Mauser in a strong bolt-action rifle comes close to matching the .270 Winchester, .280 Remington, and .284 Winchester in performance.

I've addressed the 7mm Mauser descendants, the 6mm Remington and .257 Roberts, in chapters 8 and 9, respectively. It seems that both of these great rounds have been pushed off the stage by the .243 Winchester. I am puzzled as to why they're not more popular. I don't think the 6mm Remington chambering is currently offered by any of the major firearms manufacturers. Thanks to Kimber and Ruger, the .257 Roberts is still alive and well.

When I recently visited the local gun shop, I happened to notice a new Model 70 featherweight on the shelf and asked the salesman to let me have a look. I have owned a pre-'64 Model 70 featherweight in .30-06 Springfield since 1970, and after fondling the new version, let me state that the Rifleman's Rifle is back! It was difficult handing that rifle back to the salesman.

Another topic of major concern to me is the Second Amendment. The National Rifle Association, which has been in existence since 1871, is the largest and best-qualified organization we have to fight for the preservation of the Second Amendment and to protect our right to own firearms. I fail to understand why, with an estimated 80 million legal gun owners in this country, NRA membership has been stuck at around 4 million members for so long. Also, I doubt there has ever been a more fervent champion for our cause than the NRA's executive vice president, Wayne LaPierre. For quite some time now, he has been tirelessly fighting the good fight against the anti-gunners. The threat to our right as law-abiding citizens of this great country to own firearms is as real and dangerous as ever! If you are not already a member, I strongly encourage you to join the NRA.

Well, I guess that's enough rambling. I want to close by saying that, if you are thinking of expanding your hunting experience with some varmint shooting, I hope that reading this book has convinced you this pastime will provide you with many additional enjoyable hours in the field—improving your marksmanship, as well, so when the time comes and you have larger game in your sights, odds are it will be a one-shot kill.

If you already hunt varmints, maybe you will consider trying one of the newer rifles and cartridges now offered. Also, if you are already a varmint hunter but have only used factory ammunition, I hope you will consider joining the fraternity of those who reload. It's even more rewarding when you nail that critter out at 300 yards with one of your own creations!

Related Publications

The following publications should be of interest to varmint shooters, especially to those who handload. I have included some publications in this list that are no longer current, but may still be available from places like Amazon and eBay. Up-to-date or not, they contain information about varmint rifles, cartridges, and reloading that may still be of interest today. I have indicated the older publications by including the date that they were current in parenthesis.

The ABCs of Reloading, 9th Edition
Edited by C. Rodney James
Gun Digest Books

The Accurate Varmint Rifle (1991)
By Boyd Mace
Precision Shooting, Inc.

Applied Ballistics for Long Range Shooting, 2nd Edition
By Bryan Litz

Barnes Reloading Manual Number 4
Barnes Bullets, Inc.

The Benchrest Shooting Primer
Precision Shooting Magazine

Complete Guide to Handloading, 3rd Edition (1953)
By Phillip B. Sharpe

Extreme Rifle Accuracy
By Mike Ratigan

Handloader Magazine
Wolfe Publishing Co.

Handloader's Digest, 18th Edition
Edited by Ken Ramage

Hodgdon Annual Reloading Manual
Hodgdon Powder
InterMedia Outdoors

Hornady Handbook of Cartridge Reloading, 8th Edition
Hornady Manufacturing Co.

Hunter's Guide to Long-Range Shooting
By Wayne van Zwoll
Stackpole Books

Lyman Reloading Handbook, 49th Edition
Edited by Thomas J. Griffin
Lyman Products Corporation

Metallic Cartridge Reloading, 3rd Edition (1996)
By M. L. McPherson
DBI Books

Modern Reloading, 2nd Edition
By Richard Lee
Lee Precision

Norma Reloading Manual
Norma Staff
Norma Precision AB

Nosler Reloading Guide No. 6
Nosler, Inc.

NRA Guide to Reloading
NRA Staff
National Rifle Association

Pet Loads, Complete Volume
By Ken Waters
Wolfe Publishing Co.

Precision Shooting Reloading Guide
Edited by Dave Brennan
Precision Shooting

Propellant Profiles, **5th Edition**
David Wolfe
Wolfe Publishing Co.

Sierra Rifle and Handgun Reloading Data,
5th Edition
Sierra Bullets

Speer Reloading Manual #14
Speer Bullets

Twenty-Two Caliber Varmint Rifles (**1947**)
By Charles Landis

Understanding Ballistics
By Robert Rinker

Varmint and Small Game Rifles and
Cartridges
Wolfe Publishing Co.

Varmint Hunter **Magazine**
The Varmint Hunter's Association
P.O. Box 759
Fort Pierre, SD 57532

Vihtavuori Reloading Manual, **4th Edition**
Vihtavuori Powder

Woodchucks and Woodchuck Rifles (**1951**)
By Charles Landis

Directory of Firearms Manufacturers

The following is a list of current firearms manufacturers.

Browning
1 Browning Place
Morgan, UT 84050
800-333-3288
www.browning.com

Brown Precision, Inc.
7786 Molinos Avenue
P.O. Box 270W
Los Molinos, CA 96055
www.brownprecision.com

Cooper Firearms of Montana, Inc.
P.O. Box 114
Stevensville, MT 59870
406-777-0373
www.cooperfirearms.com

CZ-USA
P.O. Box 171073
Kansas City, KS 66117-0073
800-955-4486
www.cz-usa.com

Dakota Arms
1310 Industry Road
Sturgis, SD 57785
605-347-4686
www.dakotaarms.com

H-S Precision, Inc.
1301 Turbine Drive
Rapid City, SD 57703
605-341-3006
www.hsprecision.com

Kimber America
555 Taxter Road, Suite 235
Elmsford, NY 10523
888-243-4522
www.kimberamerica.com

Marlin Firearms
P.O. Box 1871
Madison, NC 27025
800-544-8892
www.marlinfirearms.com

O. F. Mossberg & Sons
7 Grasso Avenue
North Haven, CT 06473
203-230-5300
www.mossberg.com

Nosler, Inc.
107 SW Columbia Street
Bend, OR 97702
800-285-3701
www.nosler.com

Remington Arms Co., LLC
870 Remington Drive
P.O. Box 700
Madison, NC 27025-0700
800-243-9700
www.remington.com

Sako/Tikka
Sako Limited
P.O. Box 149
FI-11101 Riihimäki
Finland
www.sako.fi

Savage Arms
100 Springdale Road
Westfield, MA 01085
413-568-7001
www.savagearms.com

Sturm, Ruger & Co., Inc.
411 Sunapee Street
Newport, NH 03773
603-865-2442
www.ruger.com

Weatherby, Inc.
1605 Commerce Way
Paso Robles, CA 93446
805-227-2600
www.weatherby.com

Winchester Repeating Arms
275 Winchester Avenue
Morgan, UT 84050-9333
800-333-3288
www.winchesterguns.com

Reloading Equipment and Components

The following is a list of current manufacturers of reloading equipment and components.

Accurate Arms Company
5891 Highway 230 West
McEwen, TN 37101
931-279-4207
www.accuratepowder.com

Alliant
P.O. Box 6
Radford, VA 24141
800-276-9337
www.alliantpowder.com

Barnes Bullets
P.O. Box 620
Mona, UT 84645
800-574-9200
www.barnesbullets.com

Bart's Custom Bullets
821 Phelps Johnson Road
Leitchfield, KY 42754
270-879-4279
www.bartsbullets.com

Berger Bullets, Inc.
4275 Palm Street
Fullerton, CA 92835
714-447-5456
www.bergerbullets.com

Berry's Manufacturing
401 North 3050 East
St. George, UT 84790
800-268-7373
www.berrysmfg.com

CCI
2299 Snake River Avenue
Lewiston, ID 83501
800-627-3640
www.cci-ammunition.com

Dillon Precision Products Inc.
8009 East Dillons Way
Scottsdale, AZ 85260-1809
800-223-4570
www.dillonprecision.com

Forster Products
310 East Lanark Avenue
Lanark, IL 61046
815-493-6360
www.forsterproducts.com

Hodgdon
6231 Robinson
Shawnee Mission, KS 66202
913-362-9455
www.hodgdon.com

Hornady Manufacturing Co.
P.O. Box 1848
Grand Island, NE 68802-1848
800-338-3220
www.hornady.com

Huntington Die Specialties
866-RELOADS
www.huntingtons.com

IMR Smokeless Powder
1080 Military Turnpike, Suite 2
Plattsburgh, NY 12901
913-362-9455
www.imrpowder.com

Johnson Design Specialties
4607 West Elderberry Avenue
Spokane, WA 99208
509-464-0697
www.quick-measure.com

K&M Precision Shooting Products
6852 Lakeshore Drive
West Olive, MI 49460
616-399-7894
www.kmshooting.com

L. E. Wilson, Inc.
P.O. Box 324
Cashmere, WA 98815
509-782-7200
www.lewilson.com

Lee Precision, Inc.
4275 Highway U
Hartford, WI 53027
262-673-3075
www.leeprecision.com

Lyman Products Corporation
475 Smith Street
Middletown, CT 06457
800-22-LYMAN
www.lymanproducts.com

Match Prep
21204 Carriage Drive
Tehachapi, CA 93561
661-822-5383
www.matchprep.com

MTM Molded Products Company
3370 Obco Court
Dayton, OH 45414
937-890-7461
www.mtmcase-gard.com

Norma Precision AB
S-670 40 Amotfors, Sweden
+46 571 315 00
www.norma.cc

Nosler, Inc.
107 SW Columbia Street
Bend, OR 97702
800-285-3701
www.nosler.com

Oehler Research, Inc.
P.O. Box 9135
Austin, TX 78766
512-327-6900
www.oehler-research.com

Quinetics Corporation
701 Hwy 281 Ste. E # 191
Marble Falls, TX 78654
830-693-0237
www.quineticscorp.com

RCBS
605 Oro Dam Boulevard East
Oroville, CA 95965
800-533-5000
www.rcbs.com

RDZ Products
P.O. Box 2132
Torrington, CT 06790
860-601-1222
www.rdzproducts.com

Redding Reloading Equipment
1089 Starr Road
Cortland, NY 13045
607-753-3331
www.redding-reloading.com

**Satern Custom
Machining, Inc.**

320 West 5th Avenue North
Estherville, IA 51334
712-362-4991
www.saternmachining.com
kimsatern@gmail.com

Shooting Chrony, Inc.
3840 East Robinson Road, PMB #298
Amherst, NY 14228
800-385-3161
www.shootingchrony.com

Sierra Bullets
P.O. Box 818
Sedalia, MO 65301
800-223-8799
www.sierrabullets.com

Sinclair International
200 South Front Street
Montezuma, IA 50171
800-717-8211
www.sinclairintl.com

Smart Reloader
Helvetica Trading USA, LLC
701 Lawton Road
Charlotte, NC 28216
800-594-2689
www.smartreloader-usa.com

Starline
1300 West Henry
Sedalia, MS 65301
800-280-6660
www.starlinebrass.com

Swift Bullet Company
P.O. Box 27
Quinter, KS 67752
785-754-3937
www.swiftbullets.com

**Tru-Square Metal
Products, Inc.**
P.O. Box 585
Auburn, WA 98071
800-225-1017
www.thumlerstumbler.com

UniqueTek, Inc.
574 East Alamo Drive
Chandler, AZ 85225
480-507-0866
www.uniquetek.com

Western Powders (Ramshot)
P.O. Box 158
Miles City, MT 59301
401-232-0422
www.ramshot.com

Zero Bullet Company, Inc.
P.O. Box 1188
Cullman, AL 35056
800-545-9376
www.zerobullets.com

Index

M
Marlin Firearms 4
Mossberg 5
My Varmint Rifles 18
 Cooper Model 21 Custom Classic 44, 55
 Cooper Model 21 Varminter 31, 37
 CZ Model 527 American 21, 55, 137
 Remington Model 700 CDL 33, 47, 64,
  65, 77, 88, 95
 Ruger Model 77 Hawkeye 8, 9, 127
 Ruger Model 77 MK II Target 8, 9, 61,
  73, 77, 79
 Ruger Model 77V xi, 17, 77, 80
 Ruger No. 1 Varminter 9, 111–112
My Varmint Rifles and Cartridges 18–19

R
Range Tests
 .204 Ruger 26–28
 .220 Swift 86–89
 .221 Remington Fireball 35–38
 .22-250 Remington 70–73
 .223 Remington 55–57
 .243 Winchester 103–105
 .257 Roberts 132–133
 6mm Remington 119–121
Remington Arms 6–7
Rifling Twist Rates for the .223
  Remington 43–44
Ruger Firearms 8–9

S
Sako 9–10
Savage Arms 10–12

T
Tikka 13
Trajectory Tables
 .204 Ruger 29–30
 .220 Swift 90–93
 .221 Remington Fireball 39–41
 .22-250 Remington 73–74
 .223 Remington 58–60
 .243 Winchester 106–110
 .257 Roberts 134–135
 6mm Remington 122–125

V
Varmint Cartridges
 .17 Hornet 12, 15–16
 .17 Remington 2, 16

.17 Remington Fireball 6, 7, 16, 37
.204 Ruger 2, 3, 4, 6, 7, 8, 9, 10,
 11, 12, 13, 16, 21–30, 137
.22 Hornet 2, 3, 12, 16, 22
.220 Swift 7, 16, 17, 61, 79–93
.221 Remington Fireball 3, 16, 31–41
.222 Remington 3, 9, 10, 12, 13, 15, 16,
 21, 31, 137
.222 Remington Magnum 16, 21, 22, 137
.22-250 Remington 2, 3, 4, 6, 7, 8, 9, 10,
 11, 13, 14, 15, 17, 61–76
.223 Remington 2, 3, 4, 5, 6, 7, 8, 9, 10, 11,
 12, 13, 14, 15, 16, 17, 18, 44–60, 137
.223 WSSM 17
.225 Winchester 15, 16, 61, 77, 106
.243 Winchester 2, 4, 6, 7, 8, 9, 10, 11,
 13, 14, 15, 17, 18, 95–110, 111, 112,
 127, 138
.243 WSSM 15, 17, 18
.25 WSSM 15, 18
.250-3000 Savage 17, 18, 61
.25-06 Remington 8, 9, 15, 18, 127
.257 Roberts xi, 1, 4, 8, 15, 18,
 11, 127–135, 137, 138
.300 WSM 18
.308 Winchester 3, 4, 6, 7, 8, 15, 17, 18, 95
6.5 Creedmoor 8, 9, 15, 18
6mm Remington 17, 88, 111–125,
 128, 137
Varmint Rifles
 Browning (see Browning)
 CZ-USA (see CZ-USA)
 Kimber (see Kimber America)
 Marlin (see Marlin Firearms)
 Mossberg (see Mossberg)
 Remington (see Remington Arms)
 Ruger (see Ruger Firearms)
 Sako (see Sako)
 Savage (see Savage Arms)
 Tikka (see Tikka)
 Weatherby (see Weatherby Rifles)
 Winchester (see Winchester
  Repeating Arms)
Vihtavuori N140 Powder 23, 64,
 79, 80, 97, 98, 113, 118, 119

W
Weatherby Rifles 14
Winchester Repeating Arms 14